New Directions for
Adult and Continuing
Education

Susan Imel
Jovita M. Ross-Gordon
COEDITORS-IN-CHIEF

Health and Wellness Concerns for Racial, Ethnic, and Sexual Minorities

Joshua C. Collins
Tonette S. Rocco
Lawrence O. Bryant

EDITORS

Number 142 • Summer 2014
Jossey-Bass
San Francisco

HEALTH AND WELLNESS CONCERNS FOR RACIAL, ETHNIC, AND SEXUAL MINORITIES
Joshua C. Collins, Tonette S. Rocco, Lawrence O. Bryant (eds)
New Directions for Adult and Continuing Education, no. 142
Susan Imel, Jovita M. Ross-Gordon, Coeditors-in-Chief

Microfilm copies of issues and articles are available in 16mm and 35mm, as well as microfiche in 105mm, through University Microfilms Inc., 300 North Zeeb Road, Ann Arbor, Michigan 48106-1346.

NEW DIRECTIONS FOR ADULT AND CONTINUING EDUCATION (ISSN 1052-2891, electronic ISSN 1536-0717) is part of The Jossey-Bass Higher and Adult Education Series and is published quarterly by Wiley Subscription Services, Inc., A Wiley Company, at Jossey-Bass, One Montgomery Street, Suite 1200, San Francisco, CA 94104-4594. POSTMASTER: Send address changes to New Directions for Adult and Continuing Education, Jossey-Bass, One Montgomery Street, Suite 1200, San Francisco, CA 94104-4594.

New Directions for Adult and Continuing Education is indexed in CIJE: Current Index to Journals in Education (ERIC); Contents Pages in Education (T&F); ERIC Database (Education Resources Information Center); Higher Education Abstracts (Claremont Graduate University); and Sociological Abstracts (CSA/CIG).

INDIVIDUAL SUBSCRIPTION RATE (in USD): $89 per year US/Can/Mex, $113 rest of world; institutional subscription rate: $311 US, $351 Can/Mex, $385 rest of world. Single copy rate: $29. Electronic only–all regions: $89 individual, $311 institutional; Print & Electronic–US: $98 individual, $357 institutional; Print & Electronic–Canada/Mexico: $98 individual, $397 institutional; Print & Electronic–Rest of World: $122 individual, $431 institutional.

EDITORIAL CORRESPONDENCE should be sent to the Coeditors-in-Chief, Susan Imel, 3076 Woodbine Place, Columbus, Ohio 43202-1341, e-mail: imel.l@osu.edu; or Jovita M. Ross-Gordon, Southwest Texas State University, CLAS Dept., 601 University Drive, San Marcos, TX 78666.

Cover photograph by Jack Hollingsworth@Photodisc

www.josseybass.com

CONTENTS

Editors' Notes*

This volume of *New Directions for Adult and Continuing Education* explores factors that have contributed to health disparities among racial, ethnic, and sexual minorities. Minority status in the United States often accompanies diminished access to education, employment, and subsequently healthcare. Limited access to education decreases access to healthcare since it is through education that individuals learn about the necessity of seeking regular and preventive healthcare, learn how to read information provided by health professionals, and research health conditions. Employment discrimination still occurs for racial, ethnic, and sexual minorities despite legal protection for some of these groups. Through employment, people become insured, and insurance provides access to healthcare that even educated people do not take advantage of when they are uninsured. Access to a good education and employment are some of the basic issues racial, ethnic, and sexual minority people face in terms of healthcare.

Another issue is the lack of research on the differences between races, ethnicities, genders, and sexual minorities in terms of disease symptoms and treatments. For instance, the lack of research and knowledge of how heart disease symptoms appear differently in African Americans than in White Americans has had very real consequences for at least one editor's family. Two of Rocco's Black male relatives have had heart disease misdiagnosed, and this caused the death of her 34-year-old nephew just days before finishing this volume. Her husband has needed open-heart surgery three times in five months for similar reasons. While she cannot prove the misdiagnoses were racially motivated, ignorance about racial differences on the part of healthcare workers has clear consequences, and there are consequences when a doctor dismisses complaints of a patient. Her husband's complaints about his health after his second surgery were dismissed by his cardiologist who told him to wait six months before returning for a check-up. If not for the nurse representing the insurance company insisting he get another opinion, he would surely have died. The second doctor stated he needed surgery again within weeks to correct the mistreatment of the first doctor. The other two editors (and many of the chapter authors) have firsthand experience with healthcare's focus on White, heterosexual, middle-class health concerns over the concerns of others, this uneven focus causing their own personal tragedies. This volume is the first to address the concern of disparities and discrimination in healthcare experienced by racial, ethnic, and sexual minorities.

This volume develops and advances strategies for understanding these disparities and promoting wellness in minority communities. The authors of the chapters in this volume highlight social forces such as racism,

---

*Dedicated to Michael T. Madry (September 29, 1979, to December 30, 2013).

New Directions for Adult and Continuing Education, no. 142, Summer 2014 © 2014 Wiley Periodicals, Inc.
Published online in Wiley Online Library (wileyonlinelibrary.com) • DOI: 10.1002/ace.20089

ethnocentrism, sexism, and homophobia, which continue to influence not only access to and quality of care but also perceptions of and trust in healthcare professionals. Several common themes emerge in the authors' work, including the importance of communication, both intentional and unintentional discriminatory structures, and perhaps most significantly, the role of culturally relevant learning sites in overcoming health and wellness concerns. Scholars, adult educators, and healthcare professionals will be interested to read about these insights. The remainder of our editors' notes provides a brief overview of each chapter's contribution to the volume.

In Chapter 1, Joshua C. Collins and Tonette S. Rocco discuss both crosscutting and divergent issues affecting healthcare access and quality for racial, ethnic, and sexual minorities. This chapter sets the tone for the volume by defining each of these minority groups and explaining, in part, the foundations of the disparities they face.

Michael L. Rowland and E. Paulette Isaac-Savage, in Chapter 2, demonstrate how powerful social institutions, such as the Black church, can play a crucial role in combating inequality and injustice in, and lack of knowledge about, the healthcare system.

In Chapter 3, Esther Prins and Angela Mooney explore how literacy and health disparities are inextricably bound, related, and even intensified within minority communities. The authors also document recommendations for addressing the issue through calculated and careful adult education interventions.

Using a postcolonial framework, in Chapter 4, John P. Egan develops his perspective as a strong ally to the Canadian Aboriginal population to paint an understanding of disease, community engagement, and the problems caused and perpetuated by a history of colonialism.

Continuing along this line of critical thought, in Chapter 5, Julie Gedro reflects on the causes and prevalence of, as well as recovery from, alcoholism among lesbians. In doing so, Gedro brings to light potential solutions for related problems among other sexual minorities.

In Chapter 6, Lawrence O. Bryant and Lorenzo Bowman weave their own perspective into Gedro's conversation by discussing tobacco use among sexual minorities, and how bar culture and targeted advertising contribute to a mounting substance abuse problem in some communities.

In Chapter 7, Joshua C. Collins and Tonette S. Rocco argue that disclosure and communication struggles are among the many factors impacting the experiences of HIV-negative gay men with autoimmune diseases. Collins and Rocco further contend that because of the gay community's focus on HIV as the premiere health concern of the community, other concerns such as autoimmune diseases are often brushed over or silenced.

Continuing on the theme of silence, in Chapter 8, Lisa M. Baumgartner examines the challenges faced by African American women with HIV/AIDS. Baumgartner argues that these women are often disregarded in the dialogue about HIV/AIDS, and that silence about the disease within their own communities can disadvantage them in the process of learning to live with it.

Finally, Lawrence O. Bryant, in Chapter 9, provides a closing perspective on partnerships and collaborations that may be leveraged to help racial, ethnic, and sexual minorities overcome health and wellness concerns such as those addressed in this volume.

As the editors, our hope for this volume is that it will illustrate some of the ways in which privilege and marginalization are manifest in healthcare. This volume aims to bring attention to a diverse and complex public health crisis that involves multiple minority communities across many contexts. The lessons learned from this volume may influence research and practice in such arenas as patient and doctor education, community engagement, adult basic education, and health education, among others.

Joshua C. Collins
Tonette S. Rocco
Lawrence O. Bryant
Editors

JOSHUA C. COLLINS is a doctoral candidate in the program for adult education and human resource development at Florida International University.

TONETTE S. ROCCO is a professor and program leader in the adult education and human resource development graduate program in the Department of Leadership and Professional Studies, and the director of the Office of Academic Writing and Publication Support at Florida International University.

LAWRENCE O. BRYANT is an assistant professor at Georgia State University, Byrdine Lewis School of Nursing and Health Profession, Department of Respiratory Therapy.

New Directions for Adult and Continuing Education • DOI: 10.1002/ace

1

This chapter situates healthcare as a concern for the field of adult education through a critique of disparities in access to healthcare, quality of care received, and caregiver services for racial, ethnic, and sexual minorities.

Disparities in Healthcare for Racial, Ethnic, and Sexual Minorities

Joshua C. Collins, Tonette S. Rocco

Individuals who identify as racial, ethnic, or sexual minorities—or some combination of the three—often experience racialized and/or heternormative oppression that can displace them from the resources and attention needed for health and wellness (Malebranche & Kissinger, 2007). These individuals are disproportionately affected by "persistent, and often increasing, health disparities" (Centers for Disease Control and Prevention, n.d., p. 1). For racial, ethnic, or sexual minorities, health and wellness concerns are inseparable from larger social problems such as racism and homophobia. It is at the crucial intersection of health and identity that adult educators sit in a unique position of privilege to promote innovative strategies to combat emerging health issues (i.e., the escalating spread of HIV/AIDS among minority women).

This chapter situates healthcare as a concern for the field of adult education through a critique of disparities in access to healthcare, quality of care received, and caregiver services for racial, ethnic, and sexual minorities. The chapter provides an overview of pertinent literature on these minorities and healthcare and explores the social issues influencing barriers to care, communication, and disclosure in medical settings. Finally, this chapter discusses issues raised by the critique of and need for a research agenda at the intersection of identity, healthcare, and adult education.

Healthcare, Minorities, and Adult Education

Health concerns often prompt individuals to seek learning and developmental opportunities so that they may learn about, facilitate, and embody behaviors that promote a healthier lifestyle (Mancuso, 2008). Yet, there is a paucity of adult education literature addressing health and wellness concerns for minorities. L. Hill's (2011) volume of *New Directions for Adult and Continuing Education*

New Directions for Adult and Continuing Education, no. 142, Summer 2014 © 2014 Wiley Periodicals, Inc.
Published online in Wiley Online Library (wileyonlinelibrary.com) • DOI: 10.1002/ace.20090

provided helpful insights into "Adult Education for Health and Wellness" as a salient issue for the field. In the monograph, Ziegahn and Ton (2011) examined issues related to cultural competency as a method for counteracting health disparities based on racial and ethnic differences. However, the authors did not address the social and behavioral issues that may contribute to health disparities among not only racial and ethnic minorities but also lesbian, gay, bisexual, transgender, or queer (LGBTQ) people. Chapters examining some issue around health education or the relationship between health and education appear in different *New Directions* issues over the years.

We searched *Adult Education Quarterly* (AEQ) for a glimpse into work done on health and wellness and marginalized populations in the field. From 1950 until 2014, 17 articles have been published in AEQ with "health" in the title. Very rarely does the work on health published in AEQ explicitly address issues for marginalized groups. Searching for articles on specific health concerns or disabilities, Rocco and Fornes (2010) found seven articles published on disability in AEQ from the period 1984 to 2005. Five of these articles were on HIV/AIDS, an illness that has largely affected certain marginalized populations. One article included an investigation of African American women's experiences with HIV/AIDS and health education; it focused on the education's cultural relevancy to African American women (Archie-Booker, Cervero, & Langone, 1999). Unfortunately, there is very little work in AEQ or in *New Directions* that investigates the health concerns of any marginalized group or includes/focuses on that group as research participants.

R. Hill's (2006) *New Directions* volume explored issues related to homophobia and heterosexism in organizations and in the field of adult education, but it did not address how the manifestation of those social problems may be related to LGBTQ health and wellness. Similarly, Egan (2005) addressed HIV/AIDS education for adults, but the volume was not specific to minority communities. Guy (1999) examined culturally relevant adult education but not specifically within the context of health concerns for minorities. Thus, while not exhaustive, this chapter and the remainder of this volume bring the field's attention to the relatively unexplored, diverse, and complex health issues in racial, ethnic, and sexual minority communities.

Minorities and Healthcare

Some research indicates that minorities are less likely to seek medical attention for illnesses (Mueller, Patil, & Boilesen, 1998); those located in rural areas are even less likely to do so. This may be in part because their communities have a different understanding of or place a different emphasis on health and healthcare utilization (Lee, Palacio, Alexandraki, Stewart, & Mooradian, 2011) and also because of attitudes toward physicians as authority or due to insurance status (Clark & Shaheen, 2010). Regardless, the increased risk and experiences of illness in minority communities contribute to greater healthcare costs, which can be extremely onerous (Gavin, 1996). These problems are likely multifaceted and not so simple to understand, especially across different types of minority groups, but there is some evidence that indicates differences in risk for and experience with prostate cancer, for example, vary across racial and ethnic identities even when access to care and socioeconomic status are the same (Wells et al., 2010). These findings indicate the importance of understanding and addressing issues that arise in various minority groups including racial, ethnic, and sexual minorities.

Racial Minorities. In the United States, the term "racial minority" is generally ascribed to anyone whose skin color precludes them from the prevailing cultural narrative of Whiteness (Wise, 2008). This typically includes Hispanics/Latinos, Blacks, Native Americans, and Asians. Racial minorities tend to experience greater instances of hospitalization for preventable conditions such as bronchitis, dehydration, pneumonia, kidney and urinary tract infections, hypertension, diabetes, and more (Gaskin & Hoffman, 2000). Racial minorities are also less likely to have access to quality health insurance and/or care (Smedley, Stith, & Nelson, 2009). Hispanics/Latinos and Blacks together represent roughly 30% of the total U.S. population (U.S. Census Bureau, 2010), and yet they also experience increased instances of high school dropout (National Center for Education Statistics, 2011) and incarceration (Federal Bureau of Prisons, 2013), exacerbating problems related to lack of knowledge about healthcare and healthy habits as well as access to quality services (Smedley et al., 2009). By comparison, less than 12% of White Americans are uninsured, while percentages for other racial groups range between roughly 30% for Hispanics/Latinos and 20% for Blacks (Todd & Sommers, 2012). These problems affect not only adults but also entire families and children. Racial minorities experience higher rates of obesity (Cossrow & Falkner, 2004) and other conditions, and racial minority children on average tend to miss more days of school (Mora, 1997). Such disparities likely contribute to a continued sense of distrust for medical authority among racial minorities (Bhopal, 1998) because many believe (and experience) that multiple systems of discrimination are set up to disenfranchise them (Harris, Gorelick, Samuels, & Bempong, 1996). Most medical professionals are White and there is a paucity of research addressing diversity in the health professions (U.S. Department of Health and Human Services, 2006); cultural competence is not often stressed. Thus, addressing issues for racial minorities is likely to stem beyond providing access to quality care and must involve education and continued efforts to build trust and influence in communities of racial minorities, communicating the value of and respect toward these communities.

Ethnic Minorities. In most contexts, the term "ethnic minority" refers to a group of people, often viewed as outsiders within their country of residence, with a common or similar ancestral history, culture, tradition, language, and collective consciousness (Chaliand, 1989). For example, Koreans living in Japan would likely be considered ethnic minorities. In the United States, the overall diversity of the population makes a strict understanding of *who is an ethnic minority* challenging, but generally ethnic minorities are those who maintain their sense of ancestral history and language at the expense of assimilating fully into *American* culture.

One ethnic minority group in the United States is Caribbean Blacks, who may share the same dark skin tones of those who identify as African Americans but come from Caribbean countries. Caribbean Blacks experience much of the same marginalization as African Americans based on their skin colors (Williams et al., 2007) but are often not fully seen as being part of African American communities (Gordon, 2007) because of language and other cultural differences. These differences may preclude them from important dialogue about healthcare and services. Further, in many Caribbean countries, healthcare does not operate the same way it does in the United States; this can be confusing for those who did not grow up in the United States and contribute to misunderstandings of the system, how doctors visits work, what services patients are financially responsible for, and more (Arthur & Katkin, 2006).

Another example is Native Americans, who experience high instances of diabetes (Burrows, Geiss, Engelgau, & Acton, 2000) and cardiovascular disease (Devereux et al., 2000) as a result of being introduced to Anglo customs, traditions, and even diseases and then marginalized to the periphery of Anglo healthcare. The conventional top-down structure of modern medical care and aid can also discourage Native Americans from seeking care because approaches of healthcare professionals disregard or mismanage Native American customs and knowledge (Mendenhall et al., 2010). As a form of oppression and discrimination, this may increasingly affect those Native Americans who do not have the social or political power to make decisions regarding their own health, such as the very young and the very old. Attitudes toward, ideas about, and trust in health and wellness in these contexts can, for these reasons and because of the history of colonialism, become incredibly complex and increasingly difficult to navigate (Goodkind et al., 2011) both for community members and for medical professionals outside the communities.

Sexual Minorities. Sexual minorities are individuals who do not identify as heterosexual (i.e., lesbians, gay men, and bisexual men and women) and/or do not identify with the gender binary of male and female (i.e., intersex or transgender people) (Heinze, 1998). Many sexual minorities experience social/familial isolation related to their sexual/gender identities at some point in their lives (Hatzenbuehler, McLaughlin, & Xuan, 2012). Such isolation, even if short-lived, can contribute to sexual minorities' sense that they are alone, can trust few others, and can lead to depression (Hatzenbuehler, Hilt, & Nolen-Hoeksema, 2010). Stigma related to sexual orientation, such as the perceived increased risk of HIV/AIDS or STI infection, and gender identity, such as assumed mental illness or instability, weakens sexual minorities' willingness to seek medical attention or consultations (Adams, McCreanor, & Braun, 2013). When sexual minorities do experience health problems or concerns unique to their community, they may be ill equipped to address them. Homophobia remains a pervasive problem in the medical professions (Jowett & Peel, 2009)

New Directions for Adult and Continuing Education • DOI: 10.1002/ace

and can affect how and if sexual minorities are treated for health and wellness problems. In addition, stress related to being a sexual minority can worsen or complicate health problems and make talking about, dealing with, and/or healing from them more difficult (Lewis, Derlega, Griffin, & Krowinski, 2003).

Social Issues in Healthcare for Minorities

Barriers to care already discussed include insurance status, knowledge of health and wellness, community attitudes toward authority or the medical community, discrimination, and trust, among others. Each of these barriers is in some ways indicative of systemic social issues that place racial, ethnic, and/or sexual minorities at the bottom of the social hierarchy. These groups are often more limited, generally in terms of access to education (O'Connor, 2010), social capital (Portes & Vickstrom, 2011), and other resources such as money (Hacker & Pierson, 2010); this limited access undoubtedly "spills" over into other areas of life. Many of these communities are concentrated in either poor urban or rural areas, thus limiting potential access to quality care from the beginning. Those minorities who have had limited access to opportunities for things like quality education, and are employed in low-paying jobs with little or no benefits, experience barriers to care for reasons such as not being able to afford a day off work to take care of themselves or a sick child or partner. Thus, health and wellness can become a secondary concern for families and communities of minorities who have never experienced a reality that says otherwise (Shi & Singh, 2009).

Communication about health and wellness also offers its own set of complicated barriers for minorities. Ethnic minorities whose first language is not English, for example, may struggle communicating effectively about health with medical professionals (Elder, Ayala, Parra-Medina, & Talavera, 2009). Sexual minorities can also struggle with communication as they battle stigma, stereotypes, and assumptions related to their sexual and gender identities (Sedgwick, 1990) or fear asking certain questions of doctors who are not also sexual minorities (Adams et al., 2013). Communication may be hindered by differences in levels of education between medical professionals and patients, community understandings about certain health conditions, prejudice, and cultural differences and in/sensitivities, but regardless of differences communication between both parties is essential (Davis, 2010). Some minorities may not feel comfortable talking about the issues they face in their communities or at home with regard to health/wellness because they fear judgmental or intransigent reactions from the receivers of the communication (Adams et al., 2013; Bhopal, 1998). These factors can make the process of getting and staying healthy much more complicated.

Racial, ethnic, and sexual minorities may all struggle with disclosure in healthcare settings to varying degrees and for different reasons. For example, sexual minorities' "minority status" is not necessarily known unless it is disclosed (Fassinger, 1991); however, "coming out" to doctors and other healthcare professionals can be an important part of sexual minorities' health and wellness (Dew, Myers, & Wightman, 2006). If a sexual minority does not perceive that her/his doctor will be accepting or understanding of her/his identity, she/he may be less likely to come out and therefore less likely to communicate about or receive advice/treatment for health issues unique to being a sexual minority (Adams et al., 2013). Thus, one major barrier to disclosure for all minorities is mis/trust. Another barrier is perceived empathy or kinship of healthcare professionals (Kai et al., 2007). Minorities of all kinds may be more comfortable disclosing personal health and wellness information to those they perceive as members of one or more of their own communities. Seeking to communicate primarily with those with whom you feel safe or familiar is a natural part of the disclosure process (Pennebaker & Francis, 1996). Finally, a third barrier to disclosure is that of terminology or common language used in minority communities. Minority communities often create and maintain a language more easily understood by fellow community members than by outsiders. For example, gay men often classify other gay men into categories such as "poz" (meaning HIV-positive). Disclosure of health and wellness issues or identity may become complicated when healthcare professionals do not share this same understanding of the language used. Thus, barriers to disclosure and therefore treatment may be as simple as the misuse or misunderstanding of certain terms or phrases.

At the Intersection of Identity and Healthcare: Implications for Adult Education

As one of the major concerns of adult education has long been identity development, or learning about the self (Chickering & Reisser, 1993), thinking about how health and wellness may intersect with minority identities in the process of growing and learning is logical. Within most communities, individuals begin to learn about their identities in relation to what those who immediately surround them think, say, and do. Thus, perhaps the most crucial implication for identity development in relation to health and wellness for racial, ethnic, and sexual minorities is that of improved or increased community education directly addressing many of the issues highlighted previously. For racial and ethnic minorities, perhaps these communities are more often than not more traditional in nature—education should take place in schools, religious institutions, families, and through already-existing educational and health services. Sexual minorities may also benefit from community education in these forums; however, in order to educate those sexual minorities who have been disowned/shunned from communities of "birth" (e.g., family), health and wellness campaigns may be more effective in resource centers and other social venues in which sexual minorities gather for fellowship. In these ways, health and wellness education can be more equitably utilized. Racial, ethnic, and sexual minorities may achieve a greater understanding of healthcare by making

New Directions for Adult and Continuing Education • DOI: 10.1002/ace

information an accessible, integrated part of daily life. Such access may change the way individuals and minority communities approach and view healthcare.

Patient education and professional development of healthcare practitioners may be improved from a deeper understanding of how health and wellness are perceived, understood, and enacted in minority communities. For healthcare practitioners, being aware of racial, ethnic, and sexual minority perceptions of health, wellness, and the healthcare process may help practitioners improve the systems designed to serve patients. These improvements could be beneficial in seeking physicians, care facilities, or information online. As discussed in this chapter, many racial, ethnic, and sexual minority individuals may opt to select healthcare professionals who they feel are sympathetic to or even a part of their own communities. Patient education may be improved by helping patients from many walks of life make these kinds of decisions and choices in an informed way, selecting the best healthcare options while remaining culturally sensitive. In the same way, healthcare professionals may benefit from training and information regarding the real concerns of minority communities. Healthcare professionals may then choose to use this information to increase knowledge, target services, hone interpersonal skills, and develop a more holistic understanding of the individuals and communities with whom they interact on a regular basis.

References

Adams, J., McCreanor, T., & Braun, V. (2013). Gay men's explanations of health and how to improve it. *Qualitative Health Research*, 23(7), 887–899.

Archie-Booker, D. E., Cervero, R. M., & Langone, C. A. (1999). The politics of planning culturally relevant AIDS prevention education for African-American women. *Adult Education Quarterly*, 49(4), 163–175.

Arthur, C. M., & Katkin, E. S. (2006). Making a case for the examination of ethnicity of Blacks in United States health research. *Journal of Health Care for the Poor and Underserved*, 17(1), 5–36.

Bhopal, R. (1998). Spectre of racism in health and health care: Lessons from history and the United States. *BMJ*, 316(7149), 1970–1973.

Burrows, N. R., Geiss, L. S., Engelgau, M. M., & Acton, K. J. (2000). Prevalence of diabetes among Native Americans and Alaska Natives, 1990–1997: An increasing burden. *Diabetes Care*, 23(12), 1786–1790.

Centers for Disease Control and Prevention (CDC). (n.d.). *OMHHE fact sheet*. CDC website. Retrieved from http://www.cdc.gov/minorityhealth/about/OMHHE.pdf

Chaliand, G. (Ed.). (1989). *Minority peoples in the age of nation-states*. London, UK: Pluto.

Chickering, A. W., & Reisser, L. (1993). *Education and identity: The Jossey-Bass higher and adult education series*. San Francisco, CA: Jossey-Bass.

Clark, L. T., & Shaheen, S. (2010). Dyslipidemia in racial/ethnic groups. In K. C. Ferdinand & A. Armani (Eds.), *Contemporary cardiology: Cardiovascular disease in racial and ethnic minorities* (pp. 119–138). New York, NY: Humana Press.

Cossrow, N., & Falkner, B. (2004). Race/ethnic issues in obesity and obesity-related co-morbidities. *Journal of Clinical Endocrinology & Metabolism*, 89(6), 2590–2594.

Davis, D. (2010). Simple but not always easy: Improving doctor–patient communication. *Journal of Communication in Healthcare*, 3(3–4), 240–245.

Devereux, R. B., Roman, M. J., Paranicas, M., O'Grady, M. J., Lee, E. T., Welty, T. K., ... Howard, B. V. (2000). Impact of diabetes on cardiac structure and function the strong heart study. *Circulation*, *101*(19), 2271–2276.

Dew, B. J., Myers, J. E., & Wightman, L. F. (2006). Wellness in adult gay males: Examining the impact of internalized homophobia, self-disclosure, and self-disclosure to parents. *Journal of LGBT Issues in Counseling*, *1*(1), 23–40.

Egan. J. P. (Ed.). (2005). *New Directions for Adult and Continuing Education: No. 105. HIV/AIDS education for adults*. San Francisco, CA: Jossey-Bass.

Elder, J. P., Ayala, G. X., Parra-Medina, D., & Talavera, G. A. (2009). Health communication in the Latino community: Issues and approaches. *Annual Review of Public Health*, *30*, 227–251.

Fassinger, R. E. (1991). The hidden minority issues and challenges in working with lesbian women and gay men. *The Counseling Psychologist*, *19*(2), 157–176.

Federal Bureau of Prisons. (2013). *Statistics*. Retrieved from http://www.bop.gov/news/quick.jsp#1

Gaskin, D. J., & Hoffman, C. (2000). Racial and ethnic differences in preventable hospitalizations across 10 states. *Medical Care Research and Review*, *57*(4), 85–107.

Gavin, J. R. (1996). Diabetes in minorities: Reflections on the medical dilemma and the healthcare crisis. *Transactions of the American Clinical and Climatological Association*, *107*, 213–225.

Goodkind, J. R., Ross-Toledo, K., John, S., Hall, J. L., Ross, L., Freeland, L., ... Lee, C. (2011). Rebuilding trust: A community, multiagency, state, and university partnership to improve behavioral health care for American Indian youth, their families, and communities. *Journal of Community Psychology*, *39*(4), 452–477.

Gordon, L. R. (2007). Thinking through identities: Black peoples, race labels, and ethnic consciousness. In Y. Shaw-Taylor (Ed.), *The other African Americans: Contemporary African and Caribbean immigrants in the United States* (pp. 69–92). Lanham, MD: Rowman & Littlefield.

Guy, T. C. (1999). Culturally relevant adult education: Key themes and common purposes. In T. C. Guy (Ed.), *New Directions for Adult and Continuing Education: No. 82. Providing culturally relevant adult education: A challenge for the twenty-first century* (pp. 93–98). San Francisco, CA: Jossey-Bass.

Hacker, J. S., & Pierson, P. (2010). Winner-take-all politics: Public policy, political organization, and the precipitous rise of top incomes in the United States. *Politics & Society*, *38*(2), 152–204.

Harris, Y., Gorelick, P. H., Samuels, P., & Bempong, I. (1996). Why African Americans may not be participating in clinical trials. *Journal of the National Medical Association*, *88*, 630–634.

Hatzenbuehler, M. L., Hilt, L. M., & Nolen-Hoeksema, S. (2010). Gender, sexual orientation, and vulnerability to depression. In J. C. Chrisler & D. R. McCreary (Eds.), *Handbook of Gender Research in Psychology* (pp. 133–151). New York, NY: Springer.

Hatzenbuehler, M. L., McLaughlin, K. A., & Xuan, Z. (2012). Social networks and risk for depressive symptoms in a national sample of sexual minority youth. *Social Science & Medicine*, *75*(7), 1184–1191.

Heinze, E. (1998). Discourses of sex: Classical, modernist, post-modernist. *Nordic Journal of International Law*, *67*(1), 37–76.

Hill, L. H. (Ed.). (2011). *New Directions for Adult and Continuing Education: No. 130. Adult education for health and wellness*. San Francisco, CA: Jossey-Bass.

Hill, R. J. (Ed.). (2006). *New Directions for Adult and Continuing Education: No. 112. Challenging homophobia and heterosexism*. San Francisco, CA: Jossey-Bass.

Jowett, A., & Peel, E. (2009). Chronic illness in non-heterosexual contexts: An online survey of experiences. *Feminism & Psychology*, *19*(4), 454–474.

Kai, J., Beavan, J., Faull, C., Dodson, L., Gill, P., & Beighton, A. (2007). Professional uncertainty and disempowerment responding to ethnic diversity in health care: A qualitative study. *PLoS Medicine, 4*(11), e323.

Lee, K., Palacio, C., Alexandraki, I., Stewart, E., & Mooradian, A. D. (2011). Increasing access to health care providers through medical home model may abolish racial disparity in diabetes care: Evidence from a cross-sectional study. *Journal of the National Medical Association, 103*(3), 250–256.

Lewis, R. J., Derlega, V. J., Griffin, J. L., & Krowinski, A. C. (2003). Stressors for gay men and lesbians: Life stress, gay-related stress, stigma consciousness, and depressive symptoms. *Journal of Social and Clinical Psychology, 22*(6), 716–729.

Malebranche, D. J., & Kissinger, P. (2007). Partner notification: A promising approach to addressing the HIV/AIDS racial disparity in the United States. *American Journal of Preventive Medicine, 33*(Suppl. 2), S86–S87.

Mancuso, J. M. (2008). Health literacy: A concept/dimensional analysis. *Nursing & Health Sciences, 10*(3), 248–255.

Mendenhall, T. J., Berge, J. M., Harper, P., GreenCrow, B., LittleWalker, N., WhiteEagle, S., & BrownOwl, S. (2010). The Family Education Diabetes Series (FEDS): Community-based participatory research with a midwestern American Indian community. *Nursing Inquiry, 17*(4), 359–372.

Mora, M. T. (1997). Attendance, schooling quality, and the demand for education of Mexican Americans, African Americans, and non-Hispanic whites. *Economics of Education Review, 16*(4), 407–418.

Mueller, K. J., Patil, K., & Boilesen, E. (1998). The role of uninsurance and race in healthcare utilization by rural minorities. *Health Services Research, 33*(3 Pt 1), 597–610.

National Center for Education Statistics. (2011). *Fast facts.* Retrieved from http://nces.ed.gov/fastfacts/display.asp?id=16

O'Connor, N. (2010). Access to higher education in the United States and the white-minority credentials gap. In F. Lazin, M. Evans, & N. Ayaram (Eds.), *Higher education and equality of opportunity: Cross-national perspectives* (pp. 41–60). Lanham, MD: Lexington Books.

Pennebaker, J. W., & Francis, M. E. (1996). Cognitive, emotional, and language processes in disclosure. *Cognition & Emotion, 10*(6), 601–626.

Portes, A., & Vickstrom, E. (2011). Diversity, social capital, and cohesion. *Annual Review of Sociology, 37*, 461–479.

Rocco, T., & Fornes, S. (2010). Perspectives on disability in adult and continuing education. In A. Rose, C. Kasworm, & J. Ross-Gordon (Eds.), *The handbook of adult and continuing education* (pp. 379–388). Thousand Oaks, CA: Sage.

Sedgwick, E. K. (1990). *Epistemology of the closet.* Los Angeles: University of California Press.

Shi, L., & Singh, D. A. (2009). *Delivering health care in America.* Sadbury, MA: Jones & Bartlett Publishers.

Smedley, B. D., Stith, A. Y., & Nelson, A. R. (Eds.). (2009). *Unequal treatment: Confronting racial and ethnic disparities in health care.* Washington, DC: National Academies Press.

Todd, S. R., & Sommers, B. D. (2012). *Overview of the uninsured in the United States: A summary of the 2012 current population survey report.* Retrieved from http://aspe.hhs.gov/health/reports/2012/uninsuredintheus/ib.shtml

U.S. Census Bureau. (2010). *State and county QuickFacts.* Retrieved from http://quickfacts.census.gov/

U.S. Department of Health and Human Services. (2006). *The rationale for diversity in the health professions: A review of the evidence.* Retrieved from http://bhpr.hrsa.gov/healthworkforce/reports/diversityreviewevidence.pdf

Wells, T. S., Bukowinski, A. T., Smith, T. C., Smith, B., Dennis, L. K., Chu, L. K., ... Ryan, M. A. (2010). Racial differences in prostate cancer risk remain among US servicemen with equal access to care. *The Prostate, 70*(7), 727–734.

Williams, D. R., Haile, R., González, H. M., Neighbors, H., Baser, R., & Jackson, J. S. (2007). The mental health of Black Caribbean immigrants: Results from the National Survey of American Life. *American Journal of Public Health, 97*(1), 52–59.

Wise, T. (2008). *White like me.* Berkeley, CA: Soft Skull Press.

Ziegahn, L., & Ton, H. (2011). Adult educators and cultural competence within health care systems: Change at the individual and structural levels. In L. H. Hill (Ed.), *New Directions for Adult and Continuing Education: No. 130. Adult education for health and wellness* (pp. 55–64). San Francisco, CA: Jossey-Bass.

JOSHUA C. COLLINS is a doctoral candidate in the program for adult education and human resource development at Florida International University.

TONETTE S. ROCCO is a professor and program leader in the adult education and human resource development graduate program in the Department of Leadership and Professional Studies, and the director of the Office of Academic Writing and Publication Support at Florida International University.

2

This chapter illustrates the role of the Black church in promoting health awareness and healthy behaviors, and in fighting health disparities.

The Black Church: Promoting Health, Fighting Disparities

Michael L. Rowland, E. Paulette Isaac-Savage

The United States is often touted as a rich nation. Despite its richness, a closer examination reveals several disparities. For example, since 2000 the African American median household income has dropped by 15% (Koechlin, 2013). Furthermore, "the unemployment rate for black workers is twice that of white workers" (Koechlin, 2013, p. 5). In addition to income, there are obvious healthcare disparities. In fact, it "has been well documented in the health care literature that there are significant health disparities among minority communities in the United States" (Rowland & Chappel-Aiken, 2012, p. 25). This is significant as adults are living longer. Also significant is the role of the Black church in attempting to address the disparities facing African Americans.

The purpose of this chapter is to examine the role of the Black church in promoting health awareness and healthy behaviors, and in fighting health disparities. The chapter will address causes of health disparities among African Americans, the role of the Black church in addressing them, and developing a multipronged approach to healthcare. The chapter will conclude with a discussion of how adult educators can play a role in developing effective educational health programs that target the diverse needs and health concerns facing the Black community. For purposes of our discussion, a Black church is defined as one whose membership is predominately African American (Isaac, Guy, & Valentine, 2001).

Health Disparities Among African Americans

Before we begin a discussion of health disparities, it is important to understand the definition of the term. A health disparity is a specific health difference linked closely to environmental, economic, and/or social disadvantage (Healthy People, 2010). The report goes on to state that these disparities "adversely affect groups of people who have systematically experienced greater obstacles to health" (para. 7) based on a number of factors including their

New Directions for Adult and Continuing Education, no. 142, Summer 2014 © 2014 Wiley Periodicals, Inc.
Published online in Wiley Online Library (wileyonlinelibrary.com) • DOI: 10.1002/ace.20091

ethnic group, socioeconomic status, and mental health, to name a few. "The sources of these disparities are complex, rooted in historic and contemporary inequities, and involve many participants at several levels" (Institute of Medicine [IOM], 2002, p. 1).

Health disparities continue to increase over the lifespan for racial and ethnic minorities and "people of color experience an earlier onset and a great severity of negative health outcomes" (IOM, 2012, p. 4). In 2011, the Centers for Disease Control reported that the life expectancy for the average American is 78.5 years, but the life expectancy for the average African American is 74.5 years.

Factors Contributing to Health Disparities

Several factors contribute to health disparities among African Americans. Factors can be *internal*, within the control of African Americans, or *external*, controlled by other individuals and systemic policies and practices. In general, factors may include:

> inadequate access to care, poor quality of care, community features (such as poverty and violence) and personal behaviors. These factors are often associated with underserved racial and ethnic minority groups, individuals who have experienced economic obstacles, those with disabilities and individuals living within medically underserved communities. (National Conference of State Legislatures, 2013, para. 2)

Internal Factors. One factor contributing to the health disparities of African Americans and other racial/ethnic minorities are feelings of mistrust toward the medical community and an unwillingness to readily accept treatment options that are proposed by a physician (LaVeist, Nickerson, & Bowie, 2000). For instance, many older African Americans still have feelings of mistrust toward the healthcare system partially as a result of the Tuskegee Syphilis Study. The Tuskegee Syphilis Study was conducted from 1932 until 1972 in Alabama. During this time almost 400 African American men were denied available treatment for syphilis in order for scientists to study the history and progression of the disease over time (Northington-Gamble, 2006). The abuse these unsuspecting African American males endured may illuminate the reasons why some African Americans are less likely to accept recommendations and treatment options proposed by physicians. Many African Americans may be more likely to discuss healthcare concerns and issues with a trusted pastor or spiritual leader as opposed to a healthcare professional. In addition, a lack of awareness of the need for routine care as well as time and financial constraints may contribute to health disparities. Furthermore, some African Americans simply lack the motivation to engage in healthy behaviors (Calvert & Isaac-Savage, 2013).

New Directions for Adult and Continuing Education • DOI: 10.1002/ace

External Factors. There are a number of external factors that contribute to healthcare disparities among African Americans. External barriers can include "the availability of healthy and affordable food options in the community, and safety issues that may deter one from exercising in the community" (Calvert & Isaac-Savage, 2013, p. 831). Physicians and other health professionals contribute to health disparities. Blair et al. (2013) reported that "clinicians' implicit bias may jeopardize their clinical relationships with black patients, which could have negative effects on other care processes" (p. 43). Stereotyping certain ethnic groups can influence a physician's recommendation for care and treatment (Green et al., 2007; Peek, Wagner, Tang, Baker, & Chin, 2011). In a research study based on real clinical encounters, van Ryn and Burke (2000) reported that when income, personality characteristics, and education were taken into consideration, doctors believed that Black patients were more likely to abuse alcohol and drugs, were less intelligent, and less likely to follow medical advice.

Institutional structures and policies contribute to health disparities. There is an "intersection of cultural and institutional racism as a critical mechanism through which racial inequities in social determinants of health not only develop, but persist" (Griffith, Johnson, Ellis, & Schulz, 2010, p. 71). Administrative policies, which restrict admission to hospitals; closure of medical facilities in urban, minority communities; and patient dumping are examples of institutional and/or structural racism that exists within hospitals (Randall, 2008) and contributes to health disparities. Griffith et al. (2010) argued that "cultural values, frameworks and meanings shape institutional policies and practices" (p. 71). Institutional racism causes racial minorities to be sent to substandard hospitals or even worse, not receive any care (Randall, 2008).

A lack of research including African Americans as study participants also contributes to the health disparities among this group. More specifically, finding African American study participants to enroll in clinical trials to enhance our knowledge of health-related issues is problematic. Some do not participate due to time constraints, institutional barriers and the perceived hassle involved, lack of trust of White researchers, and a fear of exploitation (Herring, Butler, Hall, Montgomery, & Fraser, 2010). The Tuskegee Syphilis Study, mentioned earlier, is a constant reminder of how the medical establishment has abused minorities in healthcare research. Many researchers often did not reach out to recruit African Americans for participation in clinical trials. As a result, the National Institutes of Health Revitalization Act (1993) instituted a federal mandate that any research that involves human subjects must include persons of diverse racial and ethnic backgrounds. Similarly, the Food and Drug Administration Modernization Act (1997) required that clinical drug trials must include persons of diverse racial and ethnic backgrounds.

Lack of Representation. The Sullivan Commission on Diversity in the Healthcare Workforce report, *Missing Persons: Minorities in the Health Professions* (Sullivan, 2004), points to the fact that the lack of minority health professionals compounds "the nation's persistent racial and ethnic health disparities"

(p. i). Despite the increase in racial and ethnic minorities in the U.S. population, the Commission found that the enrollment of racial and ethnic minorities in nursing, medicine, and dentistry have not kept pace with their proportion in the U.S. population. For instance, African Americans, Hispanics, and American Indians make up nearly 25% of the U.S. population, yet combined these groups make up less than 9% of all nurses, 6% of physicians, and 5% of dentists. The concern is having a healthcare workforce with little resemblance to the population they serve. The physician workforce should reflect the diversity of the United States and be culturally sensitive and aware of the health disparities impacting those of African American descent.

According to a report from the Association of American Medical Colleges (2012) on *Diversity in Medical Education*, a serious concern impacting the physician workforce is the consistent decline of African American males applying to and graduating from medical schools. Yet, Guiton, Chang, and Wilkerson (2007) have shown that medical students educated in an environment where there is diversity say they are better able to work with patients of diverse backgrounds.

According to the U.S. Census Bureau (2004), by the year 2050 almost half of the U.S. population will be members of racial or ethnic minority populations and therefore it might be logical to assume that almost half of the labor force will be comprised of individuals from racial and ethnic minority groups. If this is the case, it is imperative health professions and the educational system seriously consider how they recruit, educate, and train healthcare professionals. Furthermore, the workforce needs to be culturally and linguistically sensitive to the needs of minority populations. By establishing a healthcare workforce that is reflective of the U.S. population, numerous benefits to the healthcare system as a whole can be seen. Based on conclusions in the IOM's (2002) report, minority groups prefer to seek medical assistance in an environment where they see minority healthcare providers. Hence, this may increase the chances of African Americans seeking medical attention. Minority health providers are more likely to practice in underserved areas. This may increase the likelihood of African Americans visiting a healthcare professional. As a result, minorities "will pursue professions where they see minority role models" and "are likely to participate in research studies if they are conducted by a provider from the same minority group" (Satcher & Pamies, 2006, p. 406).

An increase in the number of minorities working in the health professions may have enormous potential and impact for the healthcare system. These dynamics are interlinked with the policy initiatives that we are confronted with in the Affordable Care Act, which will pave the way for more patients to receive needed services. This makes it even more essential that we diversify the faculties and leaders of our health professional schools and rethink our strategies related to services and programs to create a workforce who can understand and assist in the battle against healthcare disparities. We need to look at all institutions in the African American community and determine how we can harness diversity to achieve a workforce that accurately reflects the population.

New Directions for Adult and Continuing Education • DOI: 10.1002/ace

The Black Church

For the Black community, the Black church has been the epicenter. It served as the educational institution, the social justice and civil rights center, and the emotional and psychological support foundation for many in the community. As a center of the Black community, the Black church has served as a vehicle for healthcare and health promotion activities to address the health concerns, needs, and most importantly, the disparities in healthcare that plague the Black community. At a time when significant challenges in health disparities of racial and ethnic minorities persist, today's church can play an increasingly active role in promoting healthy lifestyles, healthy behaviors, and health awareness in eliminating the barriers to healthcare and health disparities. "The Black Church has strong roots in African traditions that naturally link religion and medicine in a very holistic manner" (Isaac, Rowland, & Blackwell, 2007, p. 262).

Dr. Martin Luther King Jr. (1966) once stated in a speech that "Of all the forms of inequality, injustice in healthcare is the most shocking and inhumane." This statement spoke about the health conditions in the 1960s, but could easily have relevance to health conditions and access to healthcare services today. While there have been some improvements since the 1960s, there are still serious forms of inequality and injustice plaguing our healthcare system.

As a result of the undue burden of health disparities plaguing African Americans, many Black churches have become more involved in the health and healthcare provision of their congregations. The active involvement is often related to church leadership (Isaac, 2002). In addition to spiritual and religious communication, the pastor's role in the church includes advice on health (Lumpkins, Greiner, Daley, Mabachi, & Neuhaus, 2013). It is therefore incumbent upon pastors and spiritual leaders to be knowledgeable of certain disease patterns and symptoms. To illustrate, Stansbury, Marshall, Harley, and Nelson (2010) conducted an exploration of the attitudes and knowledge of African American clergy in rural areas of Kentucky to determine their knowledge and understanding of Alzheimer's disease (AD). They concluded that African American clergy "hold a unique position as gatekeepers to the formal health and mental health systems" (p. 354). The clergy in their study acknowledged that AD was an incurable illness yet they "believed the use of prayer, biblical scripture and believing in God's will" (p. 359) provides comfort and spiritual harmony to individuals suffering from this disease. The clergy were cognizant of their role and position of influence to change their congregations' perceptions and beliefs about AD. They provided education on health issues by using health newsletters, in-services, and partnerships with health departments. Black churches in general have used a variety of techniques to combat health disparities. Pastors have reported providing health screenings for diseases such as HIV/AIDS, heart disease, hypertension, and cancer; hosting health fairs; inviting health professionals and organizations; and including

New Directions for Adult and Continuing Education • DOI: 10.1002/ace

health-related topics in sermons (Rowland & Isaac-Savage, 2013; Stansbury et al., 2010). The pastor's health intervention by way of communicating to his or her congregants "becomes not only a message from a trusted individual and one that is considered a spiritual guide but also a conduit of information from a higher authority—God" (Lumpkins et al., 2013, pp. 1096–1097). Hence, the reach of the African American clergy in the fight against health disparities should not be underestimated.

Adult Educators and the Black Church

Adult educators can play a huge role in developing healthcare initiatives and programs with the Black church that can further reduce the impact of healthcare disparities. Adult education has a long history of working for social justice and creating change in society. As medical and health information becomes increasingly more complex and requires a certain level of health literacy, adult educators can serve to design healthcare programs for those struggling to understand the complexities of health jargon. As Hill (2011) states, "Since learning is central to health, adult educators' insights regarding adult learning are critical in helping adults learn about their disease states and appropriate actions they can take" (p. 101).

Adult educators can contribute to the relief of healthcare disparities by assisting in the design and implementation of programs that address cultural competency. The definitions for cultural competency are numerous and vary widely, however, one of the more accepted definitions is by Cross (2001): "Cultural competence is a set of congruent behaviors, attitudes, and policies that come together in a system, agency or among professionals and enable that system, agency or professional to work effectively in cross-cultural situations" (para. 1). However, Betancourt, Green, and Carrillo (2002) define cultural competency in healthcare as "the ability of systems to provide care to patients with diverse values, beliefs and behaviors, including tailoring delivery to meet patients' social, cultural, and linguistic needs" (p. v).

Adult educators can facilitate and collaborate with the Black church to offer a minimedical school program within the church that provides ongoing education and information about health topics that seriously impact the Black community such as diabetes, heart disease, HIV/AIDS, hypertension, prostate cancer, breast cancer, and other diseases that seem to disproportionately affect African Americans. The minimedical schools within the Black church can also serve as an introduction to health concerns specifically related to adults within the community. Adult educators can serve as consultants to African American pastors in the planning, design, creation, and implementation of a minimedical school program to ensure that the program meets the needs and interests of the congregation by conducting a needs assessment with the congregation. By serving as a consultant and educational facilitator to the pastors, adult educators can best design educational opportunities that incorporate principles

New Directions for Adult and Continuing Education • DOI: 10.1002/ace

of adult learning to help educate and motivate African Americans about health concerns and opportunities. Adult educators can assist pastors in serving as researchers who can assist in the design of research studies to better understand the needs of the congregation and the issues most prevalent to a specific congregation. Adult educators can serve as grant writers to pastors and seek funding opportunities locally and nationally to further increase educational programs or to develop healthcare programs that may bring healthcare workers into the church to treat and aid in the reduction of health conditions prevalent among African Americans.

Pastors play a significant role in the implementation of health, mental health, and social programs in the church (Isaac, 2002). African American pastors can forge new community health partnerships and establish any number of healthcare-related and academic enrichment programs for youth. De Marco et al. (2011) noted that pastors play a key role in whether members of the church will participate in health promotion and research activities. De Marco et al. (2011) studied the readiness of Black churches to participate in health disparities research and found that "churches with a pastor who promoted the importance of good nutrition in a sermon or had a budget for health-related activities had significantly higher readiness scores than churches without such practices" (p. 960).

Healthcare institutions, agencies, and local health departments may first want to reach out to pastors to develop relationships with the church and community, which could lead to collaborative partnerships with the church in developing health programs (Rowland & Chappel-Aiken, 2012). Kotecki (2002) states, "Community partnerships between health care and Faith-Based Organizations are an effective way to reach people with health promotion strategies in the comfort of their member group" (p. 61). This supports the significance of providing learning opportunities in familiar cultural settings in particular where African Americans feel more comfortable (Isaac et al., 2001).

Conclusion

The current healthcare crisis facing the United States has had a devastating effect on the American population. However, this crisis, along with the causes and complexities of healthcare disparities, lack of a diverse healthcare workforce, lack of culturally competent care, and rising costs of healthcare all serve to disproportionately impact our most vulnerable citizens and racial/ethnic minority citizens. As adult educators with a rich history of social justice and involvement in civil rights, we can serve as instruments of change and begin to work collaboratively with the Black church as one mechanism to address and alleviate these problems. Adult educators have the knowledge and skills needed to design health prevention and healthy lifestyle programs that assist patients and churches to better understand the healthcare system and issues of health literacy. They can also design educational programs that provide culturally competent education and training to healthcare institutions and professional schools in how to best care for targeted populations who are disproportionally disadvantaged by the healthcare system. We must not overlook the Black church as a catalyst for change in health education. However, there must be a concerted effort by different stakeholders to work together to address the health disparities in the United States.

References

Association of American Medical Colleges. (2012). *Diversity in medical education: Facts and figures 2012*. Washington, DC: Author.

Betancourt, J., Green, A., & Carrillo, E. (2002). *Cultural competence in health care: Emerging frameworks and practical approaches*. Retrieved from http://www.commonwealthfund.org/usr_doc/betancourt_culturalcompetence_576.pdf

Blair, I. V., Steiner, J. F., Fairclough, D. L., Hanratty, R., Price, D. W., Hirsch, H. K., ... Havranek, E. P. (2013). Clinicians' implicit ethnic/racial bias and perceptions of care among Black and Latino patients. *Annals of Family Medicine, 11*(1), 43–52.

Calvert, W. J., & Isaac-Savage, E. P. (2013). Motivators and barriers to participating in health promotion behaviors in Black men. *Western Journal of Nursing Research, 35*(7), 829–848. doi:10.1177/0193945913480429

Centers for Disease Control. (2011). *Health disparities and inequalities report*. Retrieved from http://www.cdc.gov/minorityhealth/CHDIReport.html

Cross, T. L. (2001). *Cultural competence continuum*. Retrieved from http://www.unc.edu/~wfarrell/SOWO%20874/Readings/cultcompetencecont.htm

De Marco, M., Weiner, B., Meade, S. A., Hadley, M., Boyd, C., Goldman, M., ... Corbie-Smith, G. (2011). Assessing the readiness of Black churches to engage in health disparities research. *Journal of the National Medical Association, 103*(9–10), 960–967.

Food and Drug Administration Modernization Act of 1997, Pub. L No. 105-115 (November 21, 1997).

Green A. R., Carney D. R., Pallin, D. J., Ngo, L. H., Raymond, K. L., Lezzoni, L. I., & Banaji, M. R. (2007). Implicit bias among physicians and its prediction of thrombolysis decisions for Black and White patients. *Journal of General Internal Medicine, 22,* 1231–1238.

Griffith, D. M., Johnson, J., Ellis, K. R., & Schulz, A. J. (2010). Cultural context and a critical approach to eliminating health disparities. *Ethnicity & Disease, 20*(1), 71–76.

Guiton, G., Chang, M. J., & Wilkerson, L. (2007). Student body diversity: Relationship to medical students' experiences and attitudes. *Academic Medicine, 82*(Suppl. 10), S85–S88.

Healthy People. (2010). *Disparities*. Retrieved from http://www.healthypeople.gov/2020/about/disparitiesAbout.aspx

Herring, R. P., Butler, R., Hall, S., Montgomery, S. B., & Fraser, G. E. (2010). Recruiting Black Americans in a large cohort study: The Adventist Health Study-2 (AHS-2) design, methods, and participant characteristics. *Ethnicity & Disease, 20*(4), 437–443.

Hill, L. H. (2011). Health education as an arena for adult educators' engagement in social justice. In L. H. Hill (Ed.), *New Directions for Adult and Continuing Education: No. 130. Adult education for health and wellness* (pp. 99–104). San Francisco, CA: Jossey-Bass.

Institute of Medicine (IOM). (2002). *Unequal treatment: What health care system administrators need to know about racial and ethnic disparities in healthcare*. Retrieved from http://www.iom.edu/reports/2002/unequal-treatment-confronting-racial-and-ethnic-disparities-in-health-care.aspx

Institute of Medicine (IOM). (2012). *How far have we come in reducing health dispar-ities? Progress since 2000: Workshop summary*. Washington, DC: National Academies Press.

Isaac, P. (2002). The adult education phase of the African American church revisited. *Chris-tian Education Journal*, 6(1), 7–23.

Isaac, E. P., Guy, T., & Valentine, T. (2001). Understanding African American adult learners' motivations to learn in church-based adult education. *Adult Education Quarterly*, 52(1), 23–38.

Isaac, E. P., Rowland, M. L., & Blackwell, L. E. (2007). Fighting health disparities: The educational role of the African American church. *CrossCurrents*, 57(2), 261–265.

King, M. L., Jr. (1966, March 25). *Speech delivered at the Second National Convention of the Medical Committee for Human Rights in Chicago, Illinois*.

Koechlin, T. (2013). The rich get richer: Neoliberalism and soaring inequality in the United States. *Challenge*, 56(2), 5–30. Retrieved from http://www.metapress.com .ezproxy.umsl.edu/content/43t200003t2j3550/fulltext.pdf

Kotecki, C. N. (2002). Developing a health promotion program for faith-based communi-ties. *Holistic Nursing Practice*, 16(3), 61–69.

LaVeist, T. A., Nickerson, K. J., & Bowie, J. V. (2000). Attitudes about racism, medical mistrust, and satisfaction with care among African-American and white cardiac patients. *Medical Care Research and Review*, 57, 146–161.

Lumpkins, C. Y., Greiner, K. A., Daley, C., Mabachi, N. M., & Neuhaus, K. (2013). Pro-moting healthy behavior from the pulpit: Clergy share their perspectives on effective health communication in the African American church. *Journal of Religion and Health*, 52, 1093–1105. doi:10.1007/s10943-011-9533-1

National Conference of State Legislatures. (2013). *Disparities in health*. Retrieved from http://www.ncsl.org/research/health/health-disparities-overview.aspx

National Institutes of Health Revitalization Act. (1993). *Inclusion of women and minorities as subjects in clinical research*. Public Health Service Act sec. 492B, 42 U.S.C. sec. 289 a-2. Retrieved from http://grants.nih.gov/grants/funding/women_min/women_min.htm

Northington-Gamble, V. (2006). Trust, medical care, and racial and ethnic minorities. In D. Satcher & R. Pamies (Eds.), *Multicultural medicine and health disparities* (pp. 437–448). New York, NY: McGraw-Hill.

Peek, M. E., Wagner, J., Tang, H., Baker, D. C., & Chin, M. H. (2011). Self-reported racial/ethnic discrimination in healthcare and diabetes outcomes. *Medical Care*, 49(7), 618–625.

Randall, V. (2008). *Institutional racism in US health care*. Retrieved from http://academic .udayton.edu/Health/07HumanRights/racial01c.htm

Rowland, M. L., & Chappel-Aiken, L. (2012). Faith-based partnerships promoting health. In E. P. Isaac (Ed.), *New Directions for Adult and Continuing Education: No. 133. Expanding the boundaries of adult religious education: Strategies, techniques, and partnerships for the new millennium* (pp. 23–33). San Francisco, CA: Jossey-Bass.

Rowland, M. L., & Isaac-Savage, E. P. (2013). As I see it. A study of African American pastors' views on health and health education in the Black Church. *Journal of Religion and Health*. Advance online publication. doi:10.1007/s10943-013-9705-2

Satcher, D., & Pamies, R. J. (Eds.). (2006). *Multicultural medicine and health disparities*. New York, NY: McGraw-Hill.

Stansbury, K. L., Marshall, G. L., Harley, D. A., & Nelson, N. (2010). Rural African Amer-ican clergy: An exploration of their attitudes and knowledge of Alzheimer's disease. *Journal of Gerontological Social Work*, 53, 352–365.

Sullivan, L. W. (2004). *Missing persons: Minorities in the health professions: A report of the Sullivan Commission on Diversity in the Healthcare Workforce*. Retrieved from http://www.aacn.nche.edu/media-relations/SullivanReport.pdf

U.S. Census Bureau. (2004). *U. S. interim projections by age, sex, race, and Hispanic origin*. Retrieved from http://www.census.gov/population/projections/data/national/usinterimproj.html

van Ryn, M., & Burke, J. (2000). The effect of patient race and socio-economic status on physicians' perceptions of patients. *Social Science and Medicine, 50*(6), 813–828.

MICHAEL L. ROWLAND *is associate dean for Diversity Initiatives and Community Engagement and assistant professor at the University of Louisville School of Medicine. He is also an assistant professor in the College of Education and Human Development at the University of Louisville.*

E. PAULETTE ISAAC-SAVAGE *is a professor of adult education and program coordinator at the University of Missouri–St. Louis.*

3

This chapter explores the relationship between literacy and health disparities, focusing on the concept of health literacy. Recommendations are provided for ways to bridge the health literacy gap for learners in adult basic education and family literacy programs.

Literacy and Health Disparities

Esther Prins, Angela Mooney

The purpose of this chapter is to explore the relationship between literacy and health disparities and to suggest how educators can help bridge the health literacy (HL) gap. Over the past decade, research and policy on HL has burgeoned. For instance, one of seven goals in the 2010 *National Action Plan to Improve Health Literacy* (U.S. Department of Health and Human Services & Office of Disease Prevention and Health Promotion, 2010) is to "support and expand local efforts to provide adult education, English language instruction, and culturally and linguistically appropriate health information services in the community" (p. 35). Once the purview of medical professionals, health literacy is now considered a pertinent topic for educators, especially those working in adult education and family literacy (AEFL) programs that serve marginalized groups.

According to standardized tests, approximately 80 million U.S. adults have limited health literacy, meaning they have difficulty with the print literacy and numeracy skills needed to manage their health or that of family members (Kutner, Greenburg, Jin, & Paulsen, 2006). In sum, "Adults with limited health literacy, as measured by reading and numeracy skills, have less knowledge of disease management and of health-promoting behaviors, report poorer health status, and are less likely to use preventive services" (Nielsen-Bohlman, Panzer, & Kindig, 2004, p. 8). Low health literacy (LHL) is disproportionately prevalent among persons of color, nonnative English speakers, older adults, and people with limited income and schooling (Heinrich, 2012; Kaphingst, Goodman, Pyke, Stafford, & Lachance, 2012)—the very groups that are prevalent in AEFL programs. As such, AEFL educators can play a key role in enhancing health literacy.

Conceptualizing Health Literacy

How we define HL shapes our assumptions about what the problem is and, consequently, its solution. Historically, the dominant approach to HL focused

New Directions for Adult and Continuing Education, no. 142, Summer 2014 © 2014 Wiley Periodicals, Inc
Published online in Wiley Online Library (wileyonlinelibrary.com) • DOI: 10.1002/ace.20092

on individual, functional skills such as reading medicine labels. This "clinical" (Pleasant & Kuruvilla, 2008) or "medical literacy" approach (Peerson & Saunders, 2009) is concerned with "cognitive capabilities, skills and behaviors which reflect an individual's capacity to function in the role of a patient within the healthcare system" (Sørensen et al., 2012, p. 4). For instance, the National Library of Medicine's widely used definition states that HL is "the degree to which individuals have the capacity to obtain, process, and understand basic health information and services needed to make appropriate health decisions" (Ratzan & Parker, 2000, quoted in Nielsen-Bohlman et al., 2004, p. 2).

Recent discussions have sought to correct the shortcomings of this view, namely, that it is individualistic and narrowly focused on reading comprehension, holds individuals responsible for health outcomes, ignores societal conditions that limit access to healthcare, defines HL as a risk instead of an asset, and aims to create compliant patients (Nutbeam, 2008, 2009; Ronson & Rootman, 2012). Within a "public health" (Pleasant & Kuruvilla, 2008) or "asset" (Nutbeam, 2008) framework, HL is a dynamic social practice rooted in specific sociocultural settings (Chinn, 2011; Mårtensson & Hensing, 2012; Papen, 2009). In this view, "The onus should not be on individuals alone to solve the problem by improving their skills"; rather, healthcare professionals and organizations are also responsible for using effective oral and written communication (Ronson & Rootman, 2012, p. 109). Additionally, HL is a "shared resource," meaning that people exchange knowledge, interpret health information, and make healthcare decisions with assistance from social network members (Papen, 2009).

HL involves more than individual knowledge. *Critical* health literacy (Nutbeam, 2000) entails the ability to evaluate information, make meaning of the social determinants of health (e.g., how education, income, race, and environmental and community conditions contribute to health disparities), and collectively advocate for one's health needs and improve health outcomes for themselves and their communities (Chinn, 2011). We employ a definition of HL that incorporates functional and critical dimensions:

> Health literacy is linked to literacy and entails people's knowledge, motivation and competences [sic] to access, understand, appraise, and apply health information in order to make judgments and take decisions in everyday life concerning healthcare, disease prevention and health promotion to maintain or improve quality of life during the life course. (Sørensen et al., 2012, p. 3)

As health information and societal demands on acquiring new health-related literacies change rapidly, so too does the nature of health literacy (Kickbusch, Wait, & Maag, 2005, p. 9). For instance, the 2010 Affordable Care Act requires adults to understand complex changes in healthcare policies, rights, insurance coverage, and related information.

Beliefs about the causes of individual health literacy status are debated as much as the concept itself. Some of these precursors include "demographic, psychosocial, and cultural factors, as well as…more proximal factors such as general literacy, individual characteristics and prior experience with illness and the healthcare system" (Sørensen et al., 2012, p. 7). Health literacy and health outcomes are also shaped by sociocultural factors, including the "textually mediated" healthcare environment, professionals' power, and "institutional processes and practices" such as completing forms to explain illness (Papen, 2009), as well as social structures, such as residential segregation (Kaphingst et al., 2012) and racial discrimination (Burgess, Ding, Hargreaves, van Ryn, & Phelan, 2008), among others.

Measurement and Prevalence of Health Literacy

Results from the 2003 National Assessment of Adult Literacy (NAAL) showed that 22% of adults had basic health literacy. For instance, these respondents could find information in a document about why a person without symptoms might need testing for a particular disease (Kutner et al., 2006). Another 14% had below basic levels, such as locating a medical appointment date in a document. To measure HL, many researchers and health professionals use instruments such as the Rapid Estimate of Adult Literacy in Medicine (REALM). However, accurate determinations of HL are difficult to obtain because current instruments "primarily measure reading skills, and…not…other critical skills" (Nielsen-Bohlman et al., 2004, p. 5), such as writing, oral communication, numeracy, and critical media literacy, that adults use to obtain and interpret health information. Furthermore, these tests typically measure individual skills in isolation, ignore contextual factors that influence comprehension, and neglect skills that patients consider vital to HL, including verbal communication, assertiveness, and knowing when and where to seek health information (Jordan, Buchbinder, & Osborne, 2010). Statistics about the prevalence of low HL are sobering, yet we should recognize that test questions about health (or print) literacy "may bear no relation to people's actual everyday practices" (Hamilton & Barton, 2000, p. 383). People may have strategies for understanding written health information and navigating the healthcare system that tests cannot capture.

The shortcomings of standardized tests notwithstanding, numerous U.S. studies suggest that LHL is significantly correlated with the following demographic characteristics:

1. Low-income individuals are more likely to have LHL than higher-income persons (Kutner et al., 2006; Rothman et al., 2006). Kalichman and Rompa (2000) found that 94% of those with LHL earned less than $20,000 per year (p. 340).
2. LHL is more prevalent among adults with less than a high school education (Heinrich, 2012; Kutner et al., 2006). In one study, 79% of those with LHL had less than a high school education, compared to 50% of those with higher HL levels (Kalichman & Rompa, 2000, p. 340).

3. Latinos, African-Americans, and Native Americans are significantly more likely to have marginal or low print and health literacy skills—and worse health outcomes—than Whites and Asian Americans (Heinrich, 2012; Kutner et al., 2006; Rothman et al., 2006). For instance, even after controlling for educational attainment and other variables, 20.4% of Blacks in one study had LHL, compared to 11.7% of Whites (Chaudhry et al., 2011).

4. Adults who speak a language other than English before entering school have lower health literacy than native speakers (Kutner et al., 2006, p. 12). Struggles with language (Britigan, Murnan, & Rojas-Guyler, 2009), coupled with immigration-related stress (Coffman & Norton, 2010), hinder access to health information and services.

5. Adults over age 65 have lower HL than their younger counterparts (Kutner et al., 2006).

6. Available research indicates that LHL affects about 25% of people with HIV/AIDS and is "associated with poorer knowledge of one's HIV-related health status, poorer AIDS-related disease and treatment knowledge, and more negative healthcare perceptions and experiences" (Kalichman & Rompa, 2000, p. 337).

7. The dearth of research on HL among gay, lesbian, bisexual, or transgender groups suggests that this is an important area for future research.

These demographic factors shape HL in various ways (Adler et al., 2007). For example, poverty excludes people from the resources needed to understand health information, access services, and advocate for their health needs. Educational attainment can influence employment, income, and the ability to live in environmentally safe, resource-rich neighborhoods. Social structures such as segregation and discrimination can restrict education opportunities for racial/ethnic minorities, thus limiting development of health knowledge and skills.

LHL is not an innate deficiency, however, but the result of social exclusion that exposes some groups to "higher health risks and lower health status" (Galabuzi, 2009, p. 252). With the exception of age, these markers of social exclusion describe many learners in AEFL programs. As such, health literacy is a social justice issue that disproportionately affects marginalized groups such as those mentioned above (Hill, 2004).

Consequences of Low Health Literacy

Although the precise mechanisms of causation are debated, HL appears to have consequences for the health and well-being of individuals, families, and communities, including difficulty with completing functional tasks, such as filling out patient registration forms (Sarfaty, Turner, & Damotta, 2005, p. 305), reading and using medication labels (Sarfaty et al., 2005), interacting with healthcare professionals (Sarfaty et al., 2005), accessing insurance programs (Diehl, 2011), and identifying high-quality health information (Shaw, Huebner, Armin, Orzech, & Vivian, 2009). LHL has also been linked with health disparities. The "cumulative damage" of low socioeconomic status and social exclusion in childhood "manifests itself as disease ... and other conditions that cut life expectancy" in adults (Adler et al., 2007, p. 14). LHL exacerbates these conditions. It also creates communication difficulties between patients and providers with different racial/ethnic or linguistic backgrounds. Additionally, practitioners' and patients' cultural beliefs about disease, prevention, and treatment can lead to misunderstandings (Shaw et al., 2009), resulting in distrust of medical personnel, worsening health conditions, and even death. In sum, research suggests that limited HL is:

> consistently associated with more hospitalizations; greater use of emergency care; lower receipt of mammography screening and influenza vaccine; poorer ability to demonstrate taking medications appropriately; poorer ability to interpret labels and health messages; and, among elderly persons, poorer overall health status and higher mortality rates. Poor health literacy partially explains racial disparities in some outcomes. (Berkman, Sheridan, Donahue, Halpern, & Crotty, 2011, abstract; see also Nielsen-Bohlman et al., 2004, p. 82)

Conversely, formal (and nonformal) education can cultivate health literacy and improve health outcomes by increasing people's knowledge and trust of "information on health risks as well as how to avoid them" (Adler et al., 2007, p. 44), as in the case of smoking.

Connections to Print Literacy

The relationship between print and health literacy is not as straightforward as it appears. Ronson and Rootman (2012) summarize the relationship thus:

> General literacy ... tends to be related to health in terms of its impact on larger determinants of health such as employment and income, which in turn have an impact on exposure to health risks and life circumstances in general and on health and quality of life (Rootman & Ronson, 2005). Health literacy, on the other hand, has a more direct impact on short-term health through health behaviors and decisions. (p. 110)

Health literacy is also situation-specific (Papen, 2009). Even people who read and write with ease may have trouble understanding unfamiliar health information or knowing how to navigate the healthcare system. Moreover, most health materials "are written at reading grade levels that exceed the reading skills of an average high school graduate" (Rudd, 2007, p. S8). Although many factors influence HL, general literacy abilities increase the likelihood of understanding written health-related information. As such, print literacy is a necessary but insufficient component of health literacy.

Suggestions for Practice

Adult educators have an important role to play in enhancing HL among marginalized adults. This section describes exemplary initiatives and recommendations for practice, which include incorporating HL topics into existing curricula and collaborating with healthcare providers.

Exemplary Initiatives. Some adult educators have worked with healthcare and other professionals to develop HL curricula and programs. Initiated by adult education and healthcare professionals, Health Literacy Study Circles+ aimed to help educators "learn about research findings, analyze issues . . . , and develop mechanisms for integrating new ideas and processes into their classrooms" (Rudd, 2007, p. S9). Rather than employ an information transmission model, the project equipped teachers to collaborate on lesson plans, practice teaching techniques, and share ideas for identifying and addressing students' HL needs.

In an experimental study involving 42 ABE and ESL programs, a team of healthcare, social work, adult education, and curriculum experts created a new HL curriculum to test whether HL and general literacy skills could be effectively addressed simultaneously (Levy et al., 2008). At the end of the 42-hour intervention covering 13 health literacy objectives (e.g., identify where to get healthcare), the reading scores of students in the experimental group "increased at least as much and usually more" than those in the control group (p. 37), and their HL knowledge and skills increased even more dramatically.

The New York City Health Literacy Fellowship is a unique example of adult education–healthcare collaboration (Tassi & Ashraf, 2008). Ten first-year medical students taught eight-week literacy and health classes as volunteers. The project enhanced their understanding of the relationship between health and literacy and ways to address the issue in their practice.

Other projects have involved adult learners in developing curricula. Hohn (1998) worked with adult education student leaders to choose health topics and develop multipart programs that were taught to adult learners. Student leaders learned health information, devised teaching strategies, implemented the resulting lessons, and developed a four-part process for health education. Through this power-sharing approach, students learned valuable health information within a literacy context while also cultivating their ability to lead, take control, and address social determinants of health, such as discrimination and poverty.

Incorporate Health Literacy Into Existing Curricula. In order to support the incorporation of health literacy into existing curricula, this chapter proposes educators might be encouraged to: (a) teach health information, (b) teach general literacy skills, (c) use authentic texts, (d) build upon prior knowledge, and (e) partner with healthcare providers, facilities, and researchers.

Teach Health Information. Integrating HL into ABE/ESL instruction is congruent with several Comprehensive Adult Student Assessment Systems

(CASAS) competencies that address health (Diehl, 2011, p. 32). Lesson plans may already include health topics, such as communicating with doctors or locating health resources. Explicit health information can be added to the curriculum or integrated into literacy instruction (McKinney & Kurtz-Rossi, 2006; Virginia Adult Learning Resource Center [VALRC], 2013; Witte, 2010). Before designing lessons, educators can survey students to determine HL needs and obtain current health information from local healthcare professionals.

The following recommendations can help educators successfully teach health information. First, health topics should be interspersed throughout the curriculum rather than isolated to one unit or lesson (Levy et al., 2008). Second, to build confidence in teaching health topics, establish partnerships with healthcare practitioners and institutions (Diehl, 2004, 2011). *Rosalie's Neighborhood: Let's Smile! A Book about Dental Health* (Goodling Institute for Research in Family Literacy, 2012) is an example of collaborative curriculum development. The curriculum helps parents with limited literacy to improve reading while learning about child dental health.

Third, teach health information in a safe, culturally sensitive manner. For example, adult learners may not want to discuss private health issues in large, mixed-gender classes (Papen, 2009). Differences between and among learners' and educators' sociocultural beliefs about health, disease, wellness, and treatment should be recognized when deciding what and how to teach (Shaw et al., 2009). Educators working with African-Americans need to understand that decades of egregious mistreatment by medical researchers and providers has contributed to widespread mistrust of the medical establishment (Washington, 2008). Using unconventional educational sites (e.g., barbershops; Davis, 2011) and creating culturally relevant materials, such as fotonovelas (Hinojosa et al., 2010) and education toolkits (Rikard, Thompson, Head, McNeil, & White, 2012) may be especially effective for immigrants, African-Americans, people with HIV/AIDS, and other groups.

Teach General Literacy Skills. Educators can also teach general literacy skills that support HL. According to Papen (2009), such skills include Internet searching, critical reading and thinking, understanding visual language, such as charts and symbols, and assertiveness training. Since health literacy is a collective or "distributed" resource, educators should encourage students to share health information, resources, and strategies with each other.

Use Authentic Texts. HL instruction is most effective when it incorporates authentic texts that participants use for real-life purposes outside the classroom, such as writing and sending a letter to dispute an insurance claim. For example, teachers can use student-identified materials (medication dosage instructions, consent forms, health websites, etc.) to teach HL, literacy, and numeracy. In this way, students learn "not only how to decode and comprehend health-specific words but also what information is being conveyed by different texts and why it is important" (Nielsen-Bohlman et al., 2004, p. 157).

Build Upon Prior Knowledge. When faced with health-related tasks, adults employ various strategies, such as creating lists of questions for doctors and using the knowledge and skills of family and friends (Papen, 2009). Educators can build upon these strategies by asking learners to share them with each other and use them in role plays or health-related literacy and numeracy instruction.

Partner With Healthcare Providers, Facilities, and Researchers. Adult educators can address HL by developing partnerships with institutions, such as community-based organizations, healthcare centers, and physician groups (Diehl, 2011; Witte, 2010). Healthcare professionals may be invited to give presentations about difficult or sensitive health topics (Witte, 2010, p. 10); in turn, students can teach this information to others. Field trips to walk-in clinics, hospitals, or community health fairs provide learners with valuable information and relieve fear or discomfort with accessing healthcare sites, while also giving healthcare professionals new insights into effective communication and typical adult health questions (Witte, 2010, p. 9). In addition, adult educators can help medical personnel improve the readability of written health materials (Diehl, 2004, p. 28). Finally, educators can partner with researchers or organizations that conduct and disseminate HL research. These types of collaboration serve to "break down the institutional, cultural, and professional silos that shape the way we think and act around health and literacy issues" (Gillis, 2004, p. 17).

Conclusion

Health literacy abilities are necessary for people to flourish as "citizens, consumers, and patients" (Kickbusch et al., 2005, p. 12). The control of personal and familial healthcare depends, in part, on the ability to "access, understand, appraise, and apply health information" (Sørensen et al., 2012, p. 3). Adult educators can play a vital role in mitigating health disparities by incorporating HL into existing programs and creating new HL initiatives and curricula. In addition, further research is needed on HL needs and initiatives among LGBT groups. Finally, by emphasizing *critical* health literacy, educators can equip learners to analyze health information, navigate healthcare systems, understand the causes of health disparities, and work with others to advocate for health in their families, workplaces, and communities. Conceptualized in this way, critical health literacy efforts build on the social justice tradition in adult education, which aims to honor adults' dignity and nurture their ability to exercise control over decisions that affect them.

References

Adler, N., Stewart, J., Cohen, S., Cullen, M., Roux, A. D., Dow, W., ... Williams, D. (2007). *Reaching for a healthier life: Facts on socioeconomic status and health in the U.S.* San Francisco, CA: John D. and Catherine T. MacArthur Foundation Research Network on Socioeconomic Status and Health.

Berkman, N. D., Sheridan, S. L., Donahue, K. E., Halpern, D. J., & Crotty, K. (2011). Low health literacy and health outcomes: An updated systematic review. *Annals of Internal Medicine*, 155(2), 97–107.

Britigan, D. H., Murnan, J., & Rojas-Guyler, L. (2009). A qualitative study examining Latino functional health literacy levels and sources of health information. *Journal of Community Health*, 34(3), 222–230.

Burgess, D. J., Ding, Y., Hargreaves, M., van Ryn, M., & Phelan, S. (2008). The association between perceived discrimination and underutilization of needed medical and mental health care in a multi-ethnic community sample. *Journal of Health Care for the Poor and Underserved*, 19(3), 894–911.

Chaudhry, S. I., Krumholz, H. M., Herrin, J., Phillips, C., Butler, J., Mukerjhee, S., ... Spertus, J. (2011). Racial disparities in health literacy and access to care among patients with heart failure. *Journal of Cardiac Failure*, 17(2), 122–127.

Chinn, D. (2011). Critical health literacy: A review and critical analysis. *Social Science & Medicine*, 73(1), 60–67.

Coffman, M. J., & Norton, C. K. (2010). Demands of immigration, health literacy, and depression in recent Latino immigrants. *Home Health Care Management & Practice*, 22(2), 116–122.

Davis, O. I. (2011). (Re)framing health literacy: Transforming the culture of health in the black barbershop. *Western Journal of Black Studies*, 35(3), 176–186.

Diehl, S. J. (2004). Life skills to life saving: Health literacy in adult education. *Adult Learning*, 15(1/2), 26–29.

Diehl, S. J. (2011). Health literacy education within adult literacy instruction. In L. H. Hill (Ed.), *New Directions for Adult and Continuing Education: No. 130. Adult education for health and wellness* (pp. 29–41). San Francisco, CA: Jossey-Bass.

Galabuzi, G.-E. (2009). Social exclusion. In D. Raphael (Ed.), *Social determinants of health: Canadian perspectives* (2nd ed., pp. 252–268). Toronto, Canada: Canadian Scholars' Press.

Gillis, D. E. (2004). A community-based approach to health literacy using participatory research. *Adult Learning*, 15(1/2), 14–17.

Goodling Institute for Research in Family Literacy. (2012). *Rosalie's neighborhood: Let's smile! A book about dental health*. Retrieved from http://www.ed.psu.edu/educ /goodling-institute/family-literacy-resources/rosalies-neighborhood-lets-smile-a-book -about-dental-health.html

Hamilton, M., & Barton, D. (2000). The International Adult Literacy Survey: What does it really measure? *International Review of Education*, 46(5), 377–389.

Heinrich, C. (2012). Health literacy: The sixth vital sign. *Journal of the American Academy of Nurse Practitioners*, 24(4), 218–223.

Hill, L. H. (2004). Health literacy is a social justice issue that affects us all. *Adult Learning*, 15(1), 4–6.

Hinojosa, M. S., Hinojosa, R., Nelson, D. A., Delgado, A., Witzack, B., Gonzalez, M., ... Meurer, L. (2010). Salud de la mujer: Using fotonovelas to increase health literacy among Latinas. *Progress in Community Health Partnerships*, 4(1), 25–30.

Hohn, M. D. (1998). *Empowerment health education in adult literacy: A guide for public health and adult literacy practitioners, policy makers and funders* (Literacy Leader Fellowship Program, Vol. 3). Washington, DC: National Institute for Literacy.

Jordan, J. E., Buchbinder, R., & Osborne, R. H. (2010). Conceptualising health literacy from the patient perspective. *Patient Education and Counseling*, 79(1), 36–42.

Kalichman, S. C., & Rompa, D. (2000). Functional health literacy is associated with health status and health-related knowledge in people living with HIV-AIDS. *Journal of Acquired Immune Deficiency Syndromes*, 25(4), 337–344.

Kaphingst, K. A., Goodman, M., Pyke, O., Stafford, J., & Lachance, C. (2012). Relationship between self-reported racial composition of high school and health literacy among community health center patients. *Health Education & Behavior*, 39(1), 35–44.

Kickbusch, I., Wait, S., & Maag, D. (2005). *Navigating health: The role of health literacy.* London, UK: Alliance for Health and the Future, International Longevity Centre.

Kutner, M., Greenburg, E., Jin, Y., & Paulsen, C. (2006). *The health literacy of America's adults: Results from the 2003 National Assessment of Adult Literacy* (NCES 2006-483). Washington, DC: National Center for Education Statistics. Retrieved from http://nces.ed.gov/pubs2006/2006483.pdf

Levy, S. R., Rasher, S. P., Carter, S. D., Harris, L. M., Berbaum, M. L., Mandernach, J. B., . . . Martin, L. (2008). Health literacy curriculum works for adult basic education students. *Focus on Basics*, 9(B), 33–39.

Mårtensson, L., & Hensing, G. (2012). Health literacy—A heterogeneous phenomenon: A literature review. *Scandinavian Journal of Caring Sciences*, 26(1), 151–160.

McKinney, J., & Kurtz-Rossi, S. (2006). *Family health and literacy: A guide to easy-to-read health education materials and web sites for families.* Retrieved from http://healthliteracy.worlded.org/docs/family/fhl.pdf

Nielsen-Bohlman, L., Panzer, A. M., & Kindig, D. A. (2004). *Health literacy: A prescription to end confusion.* Washington, DC: National Academies Press.

Nutbeam, D. (2000). Health literacy as a public health goal: A challenge for contemporary health education and communication strategies into the 21st century. *Health Promotion International*, 15(3), 259–267.

Nutbeam, D. (2008). The evolving concept of health literacy. *Social Science & Medicine*, 67(12), 2072–2078.

Nutbeam, D. (2009). Defining and measuring health literacy: What can we learn from literacy studies? *International Journal of Public Health*, 54(5), 303–305.

Papen, U. (2009). Literacy, learning and health: A social practices view of health literacy. *Literacy and Numeracy Studies*, 16(2), 19–34.

Peerson, A., & Saunders, M. (2009). Health literacy revisited: What do we mean and why does it matter? *Health Promotion International*, 24(3), 285–296.

Pleasant, A., & Kuruvilla, S. (2008). A tale of two health literacies: Public health and clinical approaches to health literacy. *Health Promotion International*, 23(2), 152–159.

Rikard, R. V., Thompson, M. S., Head, R., McNeil, C., & White, C. (2012). Problem posing and cultural tailoring: Developing an HIV/AIDS health literacy toolkit with the African American community. *Health Promotion Practice*, 13(5), 626–636.

Ronson, B., & Rootman, I. (2012). Literacy and health: Implications for health and education professionals. In L. M. English (Ed.), *Adult education and health* (pp. 107–122). Toronto, Canada: University of Toronto Press.

Rothman, R. L., Housam, R., Weiss, H., Davis, D., Gregory, R., Gebretsadik, T., . . . Elasy, T. A. (2006). Patient understanding of food labels: The role of literacy and numeracy. *American Journal of Preventive Medicine*, 31(5), 391–398.

Rudd, R. E. (2007). Health literacy skills of U.S. adults. *American Journal of Health Behavior*, 31, S8–S18.

Sarfaty, M., Turner, C. H., & Damotta, E. (2005). Use of a patient assistant to facilitate medical visits for Latino patients with low health literacy. *Journal of Community Health*, 30(4), 299–307.

Shaw, S., Huebner, C., Armin, J., Orzech, K., & Vivian, J. (2009). The role of culture in health literacy and chronic disease screening and management. *Journal of Immigrant and Minority Health*, 11(6), 460–467.

Sørensen, K., Van den Broucke, S., Fullam, J., Doyle, G., Pelikan, J., Slonska, Z., & Brand, H. (2012). Health literacy and public health: A systematic review and integration of definitions and models. *BMC Public Health*, 12. doi:10.1186/1471-2458-12-80

Tassi, A., & Ashraf, F. (2008). Health literate doctors and patients: The New York City health literacy fellowship for first year medical students. *Focus on Basics*, 9(B), 3–8.

U.S. Department of Health and Human Services & Office of Disease Prevention and Health Promotion. (2010). *National action plan to improve health literacy*. Washington, DC: Author.

Virginia Adult Learning Resource Center (VALRC). (2013). *Virginia adult ESOL health literacy toolkit*. Retrieved from http://www.valrc.org/toolkit/index.html

Washington, H. A. (2008). *Medical apartheid: The dark history of medical experimentation on black Americans from colonial times to the present*. New York, NY: Doubleday.

Witte, P. G. (2010). Health literacy: Can we live without it? *Adult Basic Education and Literacy Journal*, 4(1), 3–12.

ESTHER PRINS *is an associate professor in the adult education program at The Pennsylvania State University and codirector of the Goodling Institute for Research in Family Literacy and the Institute for the Study of Adult Literacy.*

ANGELA MOONEY *is a doctoral candidate in the adult education program at Penn State and a graduate research assistant at the Goodling Institute for Research in Family Literacy.*

4

This chapter describes the intersection of colonization, disease, and community engagement, including the author's support for Aboriginal community-based HIV research.

Injection Drug Users, Aboriginality, and HIV: A Postcolonial Glance From a Strong Ally

John P. Egan

In 2010, Vancouver Canada welcomed the world to the Winter Olympic Games via an Opening Ceremony that featured aspects of pan-Canadian Indigenous culture. Singers, dancers, and drummers resplendent in both traditional and riff-traditional regalia formed a welcome circle; Coast Salish welcome poles were centerpieces of the ceremony. The Chiefs of the Lil'Wat, Squamish, Tsleil-Waututh, and Musqueam First Nations of southwestern British Columbia (upon whose traditional, shared, and unceded territories the Games would be held) sat as dignitaries alongside the heads of local, provincial, and national governments: an explicit acknowledgement of these nations' sovereignty. The emblem of the 2010 Olympic Games was Ilanaaq, an anthropomorphized version of the Inuit inukshuk. Inukshuk are placed in the Arctic to mark the presence of humans and as way finding devices: an inukshuk says both "I was here" and "follow me." In metaphoric terms, Ilanaaq marked the way to Vancouver for the Games. The impression given was that Indigenous knowledge and identity are a central part of the psyche in Canada.

This comprehensive integration of Indigenous culture was beautiful, mesmerizing, and largely aspirational. The Games offered a glimpse of a *potential* rapprochement between Aboriginal and non-Aboriginal persons in Canada, several hundred years after first contact with European settlers. The prominent Aboriginal involvement certainly improved aspects of the Aboriginal experience in British Columbia, but a great deal of dissonance occurred—and remains (Kalman-Lamb, 2012; Perry & Kang, 2012; Silver, Meletis, & Vadi, 2012). Canadian Aboriginal community is healing after more than a century of state-sponsored cultural genocide (MacDonald & Hudson, 2012): spiritually, culturally, and medically.

As a result, Aboriginal persons in Canada face disproportionate disease burdens when compared to their non-Aboriginal compatriots. This is particularly true with respect to the HIV/AIDS. These two Vancouvers—the

New Directions for Adult and Continuing Education, no. 142, Summer 2014 © 2014 Wiley Periodicals, Inc.
Published online in Wiley Online Library (wileyonlinelibrary.com) • DOI: 10.1002/ace.20093

progressive, Aboriginal-embracing metropolis as represented in 2010 versus the one where Aboriginal persons experience marginalization and vulnerability to HIV—might seem irreconcilable. In fact, they coexist.

In this chapter, I will describe this intersection of colonization, disease, and community engagement, including my support for Aboriginal community-based HIV research. I will link the colonial practices of the state to the experience of Aboriginal persons today, particularly related to HIV. My analysis here is informed by the postcolonial scholarship of Edward Said and Linda Tuhiwai Smith. Postcolonial scholarship reflects a multiplicity of experiences, cultures, contexts, and social positions. "*Post*" can be a temporal reference: societies *after* a colonial relationship are severed via political independence. Another interpretation would be "*post*" as in beyond—transcending and transgressing—the norms entrenched in colonial relations between the colonizer and the colonized. While Canada certainly is postcolonial in this former sense, I would argue that this latter interpretation better reflects the complex, iterative, and untidy decolonization work in which many Aboriginal communities engage today. This chapter specifically addresses "those researchers who work with, alongside and for communities who have chosen to identify themselves as Indigenous" (Smith, 2005, p. 5), to engage the process of decolonization. Hence the term "glance" rather than "gaze."

It is important to note that while many Aboriginal persons in Canada consider themselves Canadian, many others view "Canada" as an imposed, unjust, and ahistorical colonial structure with which they do not wish to identify. Hence the frequent use of *Aboriginal* and *Indigenous* in this chapter rather than *Canadian*.

Aboriginal Persons in British Columbia and Canada

According to Said (2005a) "imperialism was the theory, colonialism is the practice of changing the uselessly unoccupied territories of the world into useful new versions of the European metropolitan society" (p. 135). Successive European imperial regimes were established in what is today Canada, beginning in the 15th century. During these years, where various parts of Canada were under the aegis of the United Kingdom or France, land and resources were routinely expropriated from extant Aboriginal communities (Careless, 2012; Lacoursière, Provencher, & Vaugeois, 2011). With the establishment of Canada as a nation in 1867 through the latter half of the 20th century, Aboriginal persons were further deprived of their lands, families, resources, languages, culture, and dignity through the process of "nation building" (Careless, 2012; Lacoursière et al., 2011).

Toward the end of the 19th century a formal system of Aboriginal *reserves* was instituted across Canada. Reserves represent a small fraction of an Aboriginal community's traditional lands: in many instances Aboriginal communities were moved to land outside their traditional territories. Currently, around half of the Aboriginal population of British Columbia lives off-reserve:

New Directions for Adult and Continuing Education • DOI: 10.1002/ace

almost two thirds of these live in urban settings (Hare, 2003). Reserves are under the jurisdiction of the federal Government of Canada rather than the provinces in which they are located. Aboriginal persons in Canada who are legally recognized as Aboriginal (as having "status") fall under the jurisdiction of the Federal Bureau of Indian and Northern Affairs (FBINA). Aboriginal status, its entitlements and deficiencies, is governed by the Indian Act (Revised Statutes of Canada, 1985).

The notion of "status" is fraught with contradictions:

- Until 1960 voting in a Canadian federal election meant loss of status.
- Until 1985 an Aboriginal woman who married a non-Aboriginal man lost her and her children's status.
- Children born to unmarried Aboriginal women were also denied status if the father did not have status.

Loss of status meant loss of community, housing, and income, since any entitlements available through one's status are administered through the reserve system (Alcantra, 2006; MacDonald & Hudson, 2012). These restrictions have all come from the Government of Canada rather than Aboriginal communities themselves.

The reserve system was driven by the interests of Canadian European settlers, since much of the resource rich territory of Aboriginal communities was seen as "uselessly unoccupied" in need of becoming "useful" (Said, 2005a, p. 135). As a result, reserves are often far removed from prime resource sites, particularly related to hunting, fishing, or agriculture: resources upon which most Aboriginal communities were wholly reliant. Reserves were also subsequently "off-grid" when municipal services such as electricity, public transportation, sanitation, and potable water became the norm across Canada in the early 20th century. Today many reserves remain off-grid, with homes lacking water, sewage, or electricity.

The reserve system has ensured the cultural, social, and economic isolation and marginalization of those who lived on-reserve, and has effectively excluded Aboriginal persons from mainstream Canadian society. However, a more corrosive mechanism of colonialization would soon be deployed. Less than two decades after Canada gained its independence from the United Kingdom, Indian Residential Schools were created, which further derailed and undermined successive generations of Aboriginal communities for over a century.

Indian Residential Schools and Their Legacies

Viewed through a contemporary lens, the aims of the Indian Residential School (IRS) movement were designed to foment cultural genocide (MacDonald & Hudson, 2012). IRSs removed Aboriginal children from their communities and families and erased nearly all knowledge of Indigenous language, culture, and family life. The goal was to wholly assimilate generations of Aboriginal Canadians (Haig-Brown, 1988).

At Indian Residential Schools, children rarely acquired more than a modicum of literacy and numeracy and the rudiments of an employable skill (farm labor for boys; domestic work for girls). These "schools" were usually taught by persons with little or no pedagogic training; the schools rarely sought to attain the academic standards of comparable provincial schools for non-Aboriginal students. Funded by FBINA though operated under the auspices of the Roman Catholic, Anglican, or United Churches, the religious component of school life was specifically designed to disrupt and negate Aboriginal spiritual and cultural practices (Haig-Brown, 1988). Parents who did not acquiesce to sending their children to Indian Residential Schools permanently lost custody. Canada's last Indian Residential School only closed in 1996.

Emotional, spiritual, physical, and sexual abuse has been reported from IRS survivors (Haig-Brown, 1988; Muckle, 2003). Combined with an often inferior education, IRS survivors' lack of cultural and social capital meant young men and women returned to their communities unable to meaningfully participate in community life. Thus, when parenting their own children—who were also forcibly removed once they were of school age—many were ill equipped to provide nurturing and support. This cycle has affected multiple generations of Aboriginal families. Badly constructed homes and limited employment prospects (and reliance on social assistance), alongside the disruptions caused by IRSs, have made the quality of life of many living on-reserve dire. Unsurprisingly, the high school completion rate for Aboriginal youth in British Columbia is approximately 20% lower than for their non-Aboriginal peers.

For many on-reserve Aboriginal youth the answer has been to move to an urban environment, which in British Columbia often means Vancouver. Within metropolitan Vancouver itself there are nine reserves (including those of the Squamish, Tsleil-Waututh, and Musqueam) and 11 First Nations with approximately 7,500 members (Metro Vancouver, 2014). There are, however, approximately 40,000 Aboriginal persons in metropolitan Vancouver (Statistics Canada, 2006): in other words, upwards of 80% of the Aboriginal population of metropolitan Vancouver are from outside the region. Many of the challenges found on-reserve have been transferred to the urban Vancouver Aboriginal experience. Substance abuse rates, particularly drug injection, are disproportionately high in these communities. With drug injection comes a much higher risk of HIV exposure, which is why HIV disproportionately affects Aboriginal persons in Canada.

HIV/AIDS

HIV/AIDS is a disease of vulnerability. Globally, the most significant correlates of HIV risk are economic, racial, gender, or sexual inequity (UNAIDS, 2013). HIV is mostly transmitted via sexual contact during unprotected vaginal or anal intercourse, from mother to child during pregnancy and

New Directions for Adult and Continuing Education • DOI: 10.1002/ace

childbirth, or through sharing of drug injection equipment by injection drug users (UNAIDS, 2013). Research shows that a disproportionate percentage of injection drug users (IDUs) who have been infected with HIV in British Columbia are Aboriginal persons (BC Centre for Disease Control [BCCDC], 2012). In the last decade, new HIV diagnoses among IDUs have plummeted, from a peak of 156 in 2002 to 35 in 2011. Of those diagnosed in 2011 only 15 were Aboriginal men or women (BCCDC, 2012).

Although around 4% of the Canadian population is Aboriginal (with or without "status"), 8% of all persons living with HIV—and almost 13% of new HIV infections are Aboriginal (Public Health Agency of Canada [PHAC], 2012). Drug-injection-related risk accounts for over 60% of Aboriginal HIV cases, but only 14% of overall cases in Canada (PHAC, 2012). The data for British Columbia largely mirror the national trends (BCCDC, 2012).

For over 20 years, British Columbia public policies supporting specific harm reduction techniques have been prioritized based on the main vectors of HIV transmission: for sexual transmission, condom use; for injection drug use, the provision of new and unused drug paraphernalia (needles, spoons, and water). In recent years, supervised injection facilities, where drug users can inject while observed by health workers, have also been implemented. Much of this work has been done by grassroots adult educators working in the nongovernmental organization (NGO) sector. The "condition of marginality" experienced by Aboriginal IDUs and their communities also freed them from "having always to proceed with caution, afraid to overturn the applecart" (Said, 2005b, p. 380). This paradoxical freedom led to the creation of needle exchanges and supervised injection facilities.

There has been, however, significant progress in terms of reducing the number of new HIV infections related to drug injection in British Columbia. These gains have largely come from the assertive expansion of harm reduction services for IDUs. Harm reduction services, which include needle distribution, mobile primary healthcare provision, and safe injection facilities, aim to reduce the negative consequences of drug use. Two additional factors have reduced HIV rates among IDUs in British Columbia. Many drug users who are HIV positive are now on HIV treatments that reduce their viral load to "undetectable" levels, which makes them much less infectious. As well, some IDUs inject less frequently and consume drugs through other means, most notably by smoking them (BCCDC, 2012).

Aboriginal IDUs are avoiding HIV infection; persons who are infected are often living longer—and, through better access to treatment and care, are less likely to infect others (BCCDC, 2012). Regardless, the conditions under which HIV flourished in the Aboriginal community have changed very little. Too many Aboriginal families are living in poverty. Too many receive an inadequate education and experience under- or unemployment. These symptomatic legacies of colonialism—particularly of Indian Residential Schools—persist, even if outcomes related to HIV have improved. There is no evidence that rates of drug use, for example, have decreased markedly among Aboriginal persons.

These conditions were not of the making of Aboriginal community. But it is Aboriginal community—individuals and organizations—that have taken the lead in healing.

Community Response: Indigenous Knowledge

An analysis of HIV's impact on Aboriginal community cannot be ahistorical, since "ideas, cultures and histories cannot seriously be understood or studied without their force, or more precisely their configurations of power, also being studied" (Said, 1979, p. 5). Similarly, the response of a community must be unpacked in its historical context. Global news reports in the 1990s about the drug-related HIV epidemic in Vancouver garnered increased attention from researchers and government. Concomitantly, a sense that the community needed to assert itself more into the research process took root. NGOs like Vancouver Native Health agitated for formal roles in advising research teams. As NGOs shifted their focus from *advising* research processes to *driving* them, the field of HIV community-based research emerged. Community sought to develop, design, deliver, and report research findings. Over time, the importance of community-based HIV/AIDS research was recognized by the Canadian Institutes for Health Research, which began funding training awards and research grants for community-based researchers.

One of the leaders in Aboriginal community-based HIV research is the Canadian Aboriginal AIDS Network (CAAN). Established in 1997, CAAN has conducted national community-based research projects related to HIV and Aboriginal persons. CAAN's research reflects both a holistic Indigenous epistemology and social and behavioral research methods best practices. The principles of Ownership, Control, Access, and Possession of research knowledge (OCAP) underpin CAAN's comprehensive research agenda:

- Ownership: Aboriginal community retains ownership of cultural knowledge.
- Control: Aboriginal community controls research projects from start to finish, with community priorities at the fore.
- Access: Aboriginal community has the right to access to their own data.
- Possession: Data on Aboriginal community should be kept, physically, by that community. Sometimes this is referred to as *stewardship*.

CAAN has conducted research on gender, sexuality, and substance use (Barlow, Reading, Akan, Jackson, & MacLean, 2008; Jackson et al., 2008; Jackson & Reimer, 2008; Merasty, Vanderflier, Whitehawk, & Wilson, 2006; Mill et al., 2007, 2008; Reading, Barlow, & Wieman, 2009). CAAN's studies are designed to be community-relevant, culturally situated, and methodologically rigorous as a component in the process of decolonization. CAAN aims for

New Directions for Adult and Continuing Education • DOI: 10.1002/ace

impacts at the local, regional, national, and international levels, in terms of policy and practice. Thus, its research needs to be internally and externally valid.

CAAN has a significant amount of internal research capacity, but still needs to partner with other researchers to do its work. CAAN cannot, for example, apply for any research funds on its own: research funding bodies require a university-based academic to serve as a study's principal investigator. So, the normative practices of university-based research quite literally control the purse strings for the sorts of studies in which they specialize. This "configuration of power"—between working within an Indigenous epistemology and the normative practices of government-funded health research—produces sometimes challenging circumstances for conducting postcolonial research. Limits in internal community research capacity do as well, which means non-Aboriginal researchers are often needed to conduct studies.

Alcohol, Stigma, and the "Drunken Indian"

The stereotype of the "drunken Indian" remains pervasive in Canadian society, albeit less so than a decade ago. Until relatively recently, this stereotype was perceived as factual—and few interrogated why a disproportionate number of Aboriginal persons in Canada seemed to be alcoholic. This sort of "every idea or system of ideas exists somewhere, is mixed in with historical circumstances, in part of what one may very simply call 'reality'" (Said, 2005a, p. 115).

CAAN had received reports of Aboriginal persons with HIV or AIDS (APHAs) being denied access to treatment or care—including highly active antiretroviral medication (HAART), the treatment breakthrough that has led to a massive decline in AIDS deaths—because they were "drunk." Several reports were from APHAs who either had not been drinking (or using other drugs) when seeking care or who never drank or used drugs. Initially, this specific experience—APHAs being denied care or services for being "drunk" when they were sober—was the focus of the project. However, rather quickly the research broadened to include those who had perhaps been drinking or using when they sought care. CAAN takes the ethical position that to deny care or treatment to an APHA because they are drunk or high is a matter of life or death: an APHA who cannot access HAART will die from HIV. Why should intoxication be a barrier to receiving lifesaving treatment?

CAAN needed to better understand the scope of these APHA experiences; with CAAN's many member organizations providing services to APHAs, they also needed to explore the perspectives of service providers on this question of access and alcohol use. *Alcohol Use by Aboriginal Persons Living With HIV and AIDS and Its Association With Access to Care and Treatment* (CAAN, 2013) reports the findings from a groundbreaking, multiyear, mixed methods study. The study involved both surveys and key informant interviews, with both APHAs ($n = 116$) and service provider ($n = 109$) samples from across Canada.

In particular, the study focused on

- the impact of alcohol use and/or perception of alcohol use on access to services by APHAs;
- the extent to which service needs are being enhanced or compromised for APHAs who use alcohol or are perceived to be using alcohol;
- strengths and deficiencies in the provision of services in the context of substance use; and
- policy and/or practice recommendations based on the findings (CAAN, 2013).

Alcohol-related stigma is indeed a significant barrier to accessing treatment or care for APHAs in Canada. Fully 37% of APHAs reported being denied access to treatment or care for being drunk when they had not consumed drugs or alcohol. Nearly as many (33%) reported that the *fear of such stigma* led them to not seek care or treatment. Only half of service providers were "comfortable" providing care to APHAs they suspected were drunk or high, although 63% were "willing" to provide that care. These are the "historical circumstances" (Said, 2005a, p. 115) faced by many APHAs in Canada.

These data dismayed me: I would have preferred an "insignificant" finding that little (or no) alcohol-related stigma for APHAs existed. I would also have preferred that those who experienced this stigma had been consistent and assertive self-advocates when encountering stigma. And I would have preferred that service providers were unafraid of their APHA clients, sober or not. But these were not the findings of this study. But the findings themselves are now a tool in making things different.

The Strong Ally

Whatever challenges indigenous communities face within the context of colonialization, the work to remedy such challenges cannot wholly reside within said communities. It is in everyone's interest to work across differences, since "at some point there is, there has to be, dialogue across the boundaries of opposition . . . [which] means struggling to make sense of our own [indigenous] world while also attempting to transform what counts as important in the world of the powerful" (Smith, 2005, p. 39). This process of unraveling the colonized world is in everyone's interests and a shared responsibility.

I came to HIV/AIDS research with Aboriginal community somewhat reluctantly. I brought many years of activism and strong research skills to the table when I began working with CAAN. I also brought a limited, academic sense of the realities of Aboriginal life in Canada. For me, much of the earliest days of this collaboration was in the listening, learning, and questioning. However, being a partner is not always about agreeing or acquiescing. There were times where I felt the need to assert and to challenge. These times were uncomfortable for me, but inaction would have been more uncomfortable. At several moments I found myself rather circumspect about how I conducted myself in our interactions. There were times where, in discussions about rigor, my fellow non-Indigenous collaborators and I could have easily positioned ourselves as "expert" to assert how certain aspects of our method needed to be. In reality, part of our reason for being involved in this project was to craft new methodologies: precisely to show that where Indigenous and Western notions of knowledge and power intersect there are pathways to success that assert an Indigenous epistemology while producing rigorous results. This included moving beyond traditional Western ontologies and communication norms. In the end, this reflexivity made me a better researcher and collaborator.

As a queer activist, I was rather suspicious of outsiders (i.e., heterosexual persons) who engaged in our community's issues: it was through my own studies in adult education that I began to see ways in which more mainstream ideas about knowledge could be aligned with my aspiration to disrupt power, in the forms of heterocentrism, homophobia, and heteronormativity (Egan & Flavell, 2006). Working with CAAN has allowed me to see the hypocrisy—rooted in experiential fear—of that position: if I cannot trust heterosexual allies to work with me fighting homophobia, what place is there for me as an ally of Aboriginal community? Queers would not have succeeded in so many of the battles around homophobia in Canada without our allies. The queer community is not large enough to assert majority status. Our victories are shared victories. The Aboriginal and queer communities of Canada are similar in size. Aboriginal community too needs allies—strong allies.

As the first member of my family to live in Canada I feel no personal sense of guilt or shame for the hateful anti-Aboriginal policies and practices that predate my arrival in the country. I do, however, feel a profound sense of responsibility for ensuring reconciliation between Aboriginal and non-Aboriginal persons in Canada happens. Working with CAAN has afforded me a chance to substantively support Aboriginal community: Aboriginal community-based HIV research is a part of both the healing process and the process of Indigenous self-determination. Documenting what has and is happening and articulating what needs to happen to move forward as a society are important steps on this journey.

References

Alcantra, C. (2006). Indian women and the division of matrimonial real property on Canadian Indian reserves. *Canadian Journal of Women and the Law, 18*(2), 513–533.

Barlow, K. J., Reading, C. L., Akan, M., Jackson, R., & MacLean, L. (2008). *Relational care: A guide to health care and support for Aboriginal people living with HIV/AIDS.* Ottawa: Canadian Aboriginal AIDS Network.

BC Centre for Disease Control (BCCDC). (2012). *HIV in British Columbia: Annual surveillance report 2011.* Retrieved from http://www.bccdc.ca/NR/rdonlyres/54BFF7F2 -E283-4E72-BF2A-73EC2813F0D1/0/HIV_Annual_Report_2011_20111011.pdf

Canadian Aboriginal Aids Network (CAAN). (2013, March). *Alcohol use by Aboriginal persons living with HIV and AIDS and its association with access to care and treatment:*

Final research report. Ottawa: Canadian Aboriginal AIDS Network. Retrieved from http://www.addictionresearchchair.ca/wp-content/uploads/2011/10/Alcohol-report-eng-for-disc.pdf

Careless, J. M. S. (2012). *Canada: A story of challenge.* Cambridge: Cambridge University Press.

Egan, J. P., & Flavell, A. J. (2006). Towards celebration through education: Queer Canadian adult education. In T. Fenwick, T. Nesbit, & B. Spencer (Eds.), *Contexts of adult education: Canadian perspectives* (pp. 260–269). Toronto: Thompson Educational Publishing.

Haig-Brown, C. (1988). *Resistance and renewal: Surviving the Indian Residential School.* Vancouver: Arsenal.

Hare, J. (2003). Aboriginal families and Aboriginal education: Coming full circle. In J. Barman & M. Gleason (Eds.), *Children, teachers and schools in the history of British Columbia* (2nd ed., pp. 411–430). Calgary: Detseling Enterprises.

Jackson, R., Cain, R., Prentice, T., Collins, E., Mill, J., & Barlow, K. (2008). *Depression among Aboriginal people living with HIV/AIDS: Research report.* Ottawa: Canadian Aboriginal AIDS Network.

Jackson, R., & Reimer, G. (2008). *Canadian Aboriginal people living with HIV/AIDS: Care, treatment and support issues.* Ottawa: Canadian Aboriginal AIDS Network.

Kalman-Lamb, N. (2012). A portrait of this country: Whiteness, indigineity, multiculturalism and the Vancouver opening ceremonies. *Topia, 27*(Spring), 5–27.

Lacoursière, J., Provencher, J., & Vaugeois, D. (2011). *Canada-Québec: 1534–2010.* Montréal: Septentrion.

MacDonald, D. B., & Hudson, G. (2012). The genocide question and Indian Residential Schools in Canada. *Canadian Journal of Political Science, 45*(2), 427–449.

Merasty, C., Vanderflier, D., Whitehawk, C., & Wilson, A. (2006). *Addressing homophobia in relation to HIV/AIDS in Aboriginal communities.* Ottawa: Canadian Aboriginal AIDS Network.

Metro Vancouver. (2014, January). *Metro Vancouver's profile of First Nations: January 2014.* Retrieved from http://www.metrovancouver.org/region/aboriginal/Aboriginal%20Affairs%20documents/ProfileOfFirstNationsJanuary2014.pdf

Mill, J., Archibald, C., Wong, T., Jackson, R., Worthington, C., Myers, T., ... Sommerfeldt, S. (2008). *The diagnosis and care of HIV infection in Canadian Aboriginal youth: Final report.* Ottawa: Canadian Aboriginal AIDS Network.

Mill, J., Austin, W., Chaw-Kant, J., Dumont-Smith, C., Edwards, N., Groft, J., ... Reintjes, F. (2007). *The influence of stigma on access to health services by persons with HIV illness: Final report.* Ottawa: Canadian Aboriginal AIDS Network.

Muckle, R. J. (2003). *The First Nations of British Columbia.* Vancouver: UBC Press.

Perry, K. E., & Kang, H. H. (2012). When symbols clash: Legitimacy, legality and the 2010 Winter Olympics. *Mass Communication and Society, 15*(4), 578–597.

Public Health Agency of Canada (PHAC). (2012). At a glance—*HIV and AIDS in Canada: Surveillance report to December 31st, 2011.* Retrieved from http://www.catie.ca/sites/default/files/PHAC HIV-AIDS 2011%20Report_Eng-Fr.pdf

Reading, C. L., Barlow, K., & Wieman, C. (2009). *Our search for safe spaces: A qualitative study of the role of sexual violence in the lives of Aboriginal women living with HIV/AIDS.* Ottawa: Canadian Aboriginal AIDS Network.

Revised Statutes of Canada (RSC). (1985). *Indian Act.* C. I-5.

Said, E. W. (1979). *Orientalism.* New York: Vintage Books.

Said, E. W. (2005a). Zionism from the standpoint of its victims. In E. W. Said, M. Bayoumi, & A. Rubin (Eds.), *The Edward Said Reader* (1st ed., pp. 114–168). New York: Vintage Books.

Said, E. W. (2005b). Intellectual exile: Expatriates and marginals. In E. W. Said, M. Bayoumi, & A. Rubin (Eds.), *The Edward Said Reader* (1st ed., pp. 368–381). New York: Vintage Books.

Silver, J. J., Meletis, Z. A., & Vadi, P. (2012). Complex context: Aboriginal participation in hosting the Vancouver 2010 Winter Olympic and Paralympic Games. *Leisure Studies*, *31*(3), 291–308.

Smith, L. T. (2005). *Decolonizing methodologies*. London: Zed Books.

Statistics Canada. (2006). *Aboriginal identity population by age groups, median age and sex, 2006 counts for both sexes, for Canada and census metropolitan areas and census agglomerations—20% sample data*. Retrieved from http://www12.statcan.ca/census -recensement/2006/dp-pd/hlt/97-558/pages/page.cfm?Lang=E&Geo=CMA&Code =01&Table=2&Data=Count&Sex=1&Abor=1&StartRec=1&Sort=2&Display=Page

UNAIDS. (2013). *UNAIDS report on the global AIDS epidemic 2013*. Geneva: UN-AIDS. Retrieved from http://www.unaids.org/en/media/unaids/contentassets/documents /epidemiology/2013/gr2013/UNAIDS_Global_Report_2013_en.pdf

John P. Egan is the director of the Learning Technology Unit and senior lecturer in the Faculty of Medical and Health Sciences at the University of Auckland.

This chapter explores the issues involved in the relationship between lesbianism and alcoholism. It examines the constellation of health and related problems created by alcoholism, and it critically interrogates the societal factors that contribute to the disproportionately high rates of alcoholism among lesbians by exploring the antecedents and consequences of alcoholism.

5

Alcoholism and Lesbians

Julie Gedro

Alcoholism is a problem in the United States among the general population (Gedro, Mercer, & Iodice, 2012) and it is particularly problematic in the lesbian population. Lesbians face challenges in establishing their identity, in negotiating life as "outsiders," and in relating to each other as a community (Ettore, 2005; Gedro, 2006). As a double (at a minimum) minority, and part of a historically stigmatized population in the United States, lesbians face particular types of pressures that include heterosexism, homophobia, sexism, and invisibility. These factors, which marginalize lesbians, serve as catalysts for alcohol use and abuse, and alcoholism among lesbians.

This chapter explores the issues involved in the relationship between lesbianism and alcoholism. It examines the constellation of health and related problems created by alcoholism, and it critically interrogates the societal factors that contribute to the disproportionately high rates of alcoholism among lesbians by exploring the antecedents and consequences of alcoholism. The underlying orientation of this chapter accepts the disease model of alcoholism, which is supported by the fact that alcoholism is listed in the Diagnostic and Statistical Manual, as well as the International Classification of Diseases (NIAAA, 1995). Factors such as marginalization, stigmatization, and stress place lesbians at higher risks for alcoholism than the general population. This presents unique opportunities for adult educators, who can serve as agents of education, sensitivity, and awareness to help reduce stigma against lesbians in society, and also for counselors and related professionals to more skillfully work with lesbians who are alcoholics or at risk for alcoholism.

NEW DIRECTIONS FOR ADULT AND CONTINUING EDUCATION, no. 142, Summer 2014 © 2014 Wiley Periodicals, Inc.
Published online in Wiley Online Library (wileyonlinelibrary.com) • DOI: 10.1002/ace.20094

Definition of Alcoholism

Despite the research and resources dedicated to studying alcoholism, it remains a multifaceted and often misunderstood problem that has deleterious personal and societal consequences. Brewer (2006) characterized alcoholism as a maladaptive pattern of drinking that results in great physical, psychological, and social problems. One hallmark of alcoholism is an inability to stop drinking once drinking has begun, and afflicted persons are often unable to cease drinking alcohol despite continued negative consequences in every aspect of their existence (Brewer, 2006). The National Institute on Alcohol Abuse and Alcoholism (NIAAA) explains that alcoholism is an extreme form of "alcohol use disorders." According to the NIAAA, alcohol use disorders are characterized by craving, loss of control, physical dependence, and tolerance (NIAAA, 2013a). A *craving* is a strong need or a strong urge to drink. *Loss of control* means that one is unable to stop drinking once drinking has begun. *Physical dependence* means that when an alcoholic stops drinking, he or she suffers withdrawal symptoms such as nausea, shaking, sweating, or anxiety. *Tolerance* means that an alcoholic needs to consume increasing amounts of alcohol in order to achieve the same effect. Alcoholism is a chronic and often fatal disease. The DSM-IV criteria for alcohol abuse are: hazardous use of alcohol, problems with the law, the failure to fulfill roles and obligations, and the continued use of alcohol, despite relationship or interpersonal problems (Hasin, Van Rossem, McCloud, & Endicott, 1997).

According to the National Comorbidity Survey Replication, which is a nationally representative U.S. survey, it is estimated that the lifetime prevalence of alcohol abuse is 13% (Green & Feinstein, 2012). "Alcohol and drug dependence are prevalent problems in the U.S. and major public health concerns that affect individuals, families and communities" (Green & Feinstein, 2012, p. 265). Furthermore, alcoholism is a costly disease, affecting health and wellness for those it afflicts (Gedro et al., 2012) and creating collateral damage in the form of healthcare costs, workplace productivity, criminal justice expenses, and motor vehicle crashes (Centers for Disease Control and Prevention [CDC], 2013). Excessive drinking cost the United States $223.5 billion in 2006 (CDC, 2013).

Models of Treatment for Alcoholism

There are a variety of perspectives about alcoholism as a *disease*, versus alcoholism as a *personal weakness*, and this variety results in differing and sometimes contested views about alcoholism and recovery. The American Medical Association provides resources for physicians to discern when they feel that a patient has a problem with chronic and health-impairing alcohol use, if the patient is *abusing* alcohol (NIAAA, 2005). This resource recommends that for patients who have alcohol use disorders, abstinence is the "safest course" (p. 11).

New Directions for Adult and Continuing Education • DOI: 10.1002/ace

There are a variety of ways that someone who is afflicted with alcoholism can pursue recovery. Self-help groups such as Alcoholics Anonymous (AA) "outlines 12 consecutive activities, or steps that alcoholics should achieve during the recovery process" (NIAAA, 2000, para. 2). Psychosocial therapies include motivational enhancement therapy, which "begins with the assumption that the responsibility and capacity for change lie within the client" (NIAAA, 2000, para. 6). Couples therapy is another treatment modality in which the involvement of the nonalcoholic spouse engages with the process of recovery for the drinking spouse, and learns and rehearses a relapse prevention plan (NIAAA, 2000, para. 2). Finally, brief intervention is a treatment modality in which a primary care physician or nursing staff provides information to the alcoholic about the adverse consequences of drinking and provides practical advice about how to achieve moderation or abstinence (NIAAA, 2000).

Lesbians and Alcoholism

The primary challenge facing lesbians who are either at risk for developing alcoholism, or are suffering from alcoholism, is the lack of visibility and awareness of them as a discrete population. Lesbians are sexual minorities, and they are gender minorities. Lesbians are subsumed into the category of "women" and seen only as gender minorities for purposes of population statistics on alcohol. To be specific, the National Institute on Alcohol Abuse and Alcoholism presents drinking statistics (NIAAA, 2013b) that have two categories: *Women* and *Men*. There are no distinctions made between heterosexual women and lesbians, and between heterosexual and gay men. There are no categories for bisexual or transgender men and women. The oversimplification of data presentation is emblematic of the persistent marginalization of sexual minorities. In particular, lesbians face double minority stress as women and as lesbians. Lesbians have higher risks for alcoholism than gay men (Bux, 1996, in Green & Feinstein, 2012) and lesbians "appear to have higher rates of alcoholism than do heterosexual women" (Becker & Walton-Moss, 2001, p. 16).

Saghir and Robins (1973) posited that lesbians have alcoholism rates that are three times the rates of the general population. Swallow (1983, in Faderman, 1991) said that "38 percent of all lesbians are alcoholics and another 30 percent are problem drinkers" (p. 282). However, evidence that refutes this claim has since been presented in no small part because of the identification of the methodological limitations of the study (Herbert, Hunt, & Dell, 1994; Parks & Hughes, 2005) "such as the recruitment of participants from bars ..." (Bux 1996, in Green & Feinstein, 2012, p. 266). Even though more recent research has found "overall lower rates of heavy drinking among lesbians" (Parks & Hughes, 2005, p. 32), lesbians do have higher rates of alcohol-related problems (Parks & Hughes, 2005). Hughes and Wilsnack (1997, as cited in Hughes, 2003) provided insights around the methodological limitations of research on lesbians and alcoholism that also included small homogenous samples, inconsistent use of definitions of sexual orientation, lack of appropriate control or comparison groups, and an absence of standard measures of drinking and drinking-related problems. Nevertheless, even though Hughes contests the claim that lesbians have approximately 30% greater rates of alcoholism than the heterosexual population, she does confirm that lesbians tend to be more likely to experience problems related to alcohol. No matter the methodological debates among research and researchers, whether the accepted rate is 30%, or whether it is a smaller number, lesbians have higher rates of alcohol use than heterosexual women (Kerby, Wilson, Nicholson, & White, 2005) and Hughes's (2003) study found that "lesbians were significantly more likely than heterosexual women to report having experienced one or more adverse drinking consequences...and a greater proportion of lesbians than heterosexual women reported one or more dependence symptoms" (p. 1751). There is an absence of conclusive findings that establish the reasons for higher rates of problem drinking among lesbians and it is likely, instead, that a constellation of factors provides such explanation. A fundamental explanation could reasonably be that the minority status of lesbians in society, and all that results from that status, creates the conditions around which lesbians engage in drinking behaviors that can lead to alcohol abuse and alcoholism. The fact that lesbian life has historically been organized around lesbian bars, where lesbians can find each other as well as enjoy a safe haven (particularly in the post-Stonewall era, as police raids on lesbian and gay bars were less acceptable and less routine), has been a major factor explaining the risk of alcohol use and abuse, and alcoholism. In concert with bar culture as an explanatory factor, the stress of being a stigmatized minority plays a significant role as well.

Alcoholism's deleterious consequences, which include health, relationship, legal, financial, career, and other related problems, affect lesbians just as they affect other demographics. In terms of consequences, then, alcoholism could be considered an "equal opportunity disease." There is an unevenness, however, with respect to lesbians' *risks* for alcoholism, and their *challenges* with respect to achieving and maintaining sobriety. Lesbians face higher risks for alcoholism, they have higher rates of alcoholism than the general population, and they face particular challenges with respect to negotiating sobriety (Anderson & Henderson, 1985; Bobbe, 2002). There are two fundamental challenges for lesbians to strive for recovery from alcoholism. First, there is the challenge of identifying other lesbians in order to access social support, friendship, and romance in contexts that are not framed by alcohol consumption such as happy hours, parties, or similar contexts that have copious amounts of alcohol consumption or have alcohol-related themes. Because of the relative importance of the bar as an organizing aspect of social life, for example, a lesbian who strives for recovery from alcoholism, particularly one who is early in recovery, faces the daunting task of negotiating the tension between distancing herself from bars, and the inherent resulting possibility of distancing from lesbians. Although, certainly, engagement in bars and bar culture is not the only way to meet and socialize with other lesbians; however, a lesbian bar provides a "shortcut" way of meeting other lesbians, since they are a small population,

New Directions for Adult and Continuing Education • DOI: 10.1002/ace

and one that is not necessarily easy to identify or locate. Without physically defining attributes (Barnard, 2005) that distinguish them as members of this minority group, it is difficult for lesbians to identify other lesbians in locations of general social space such as restaurants, parks, theatres, and even mundane locations of daily modern living such as grocery stores and shopping malls. This means that being a lesbian presents an array of difficulties with respect to negotiating connection with other lesbians. A lesbian bar presents a relatively uncomplicated way of identifying other lesbians because, although it is certainly possible if not likely that a lesbian bar might have patrons who are not lesbians, lesbian bars are patronized by lesbians. Going to a lesbian bar has historically presented an element of self-selection and identification:

> Not only were American lesbians without a history such as helped to guide other minority groups, but they were also without a geography: there were no lesbian ghettos where they could be assured of meeting others like themselves and being accepted precisely for that attribute that the outside world shunned. There was little to inherit from the past in terms of safe turf, through safe turf was crucial to lesbians as a despised minority. (Faderman, 1991, p. 161)

Second, there is the challenge of identifying safe, lesbian-friendly resources such as counselors, Alcoholics Anonymous meetings, and other related resources that provide environments that foster and encourage success in sobriety.

There are several reasons that lesbians are at "elevated risk for heavy drinking and alcohol-related problems compared to heterosexuals" (Green & Feinstein, 2012, p. 266). Because of the homophobia and heterosexism of the larger society, lesbians face pressures and a constellation of difficult choices related to their sexual minority status. To be clear, other sexual minorities, such as gay men, bisexuals, and transgender people face challenges and pressures. As such, they have their own particular considerations with respect to alcoholism. Because the focus of this chapter is on lesbians and alcoholism, it is beyond the scope of the chapter to explore these other populations. The risk factors, or the antecedents of alcoholism among lesbians which elevate their risk, include the centrality of the lesbian bar in lesbian life, internalized homophobia and heterosexism, which result in internalized shame and minority stress (Green & Feinstein, 2012). The consequences of alcoholism among lesbians include health and wellness, career, financial, legal, and interpersonal issues.

Stigma. Goffman (1963) is widely credited with conceptualizing and defining the term stigma. According to Goffman, society creates categories that specify attributes that are considered natural and normal, and people use these normative expectations as a benchmark around which they measure strangers. When that stranger has an attribute that is undesirable, then that person is perceived to be weak, or discounted. When such weakness or shortcoming has an intensely discrediting effect, it is considered a stigma. Lesbians, who are women with same-sex romantic affiliation, suffer the stigma borne by their presence in a society pervaded by the assumption that heterosexuality is what is normal and natural. Gedro, Cervero, and Johnson-Bailey (2004) noted that "To be same sex oriented in a society that is undergirded by the heterosexual assumption is a stigma" (p. 181). Hatzenbuehler (2009) noted that the social stigma of homosexuality, which perpetuates chronic experiences of discrimination and rejection among sexual minorities, results in their hyper vigilance around disclosure, or coming out. The constant monitoring of one's behavior, speech, and mannerisms, which can serve as signals of sexual identity, presents mental and emotional stress. Were it not a stigma to be a sexual minority, the stress of this constellation of decisions around disclosure would not exist. Therefore, stigmatization leads to negotiation of one's identity and decisions around disclosure, which lead to stress. Borden (2007) observed that "despite our modern understanding of alcoholism as a disease, and a growing acceptance of gay people in our society, stigmas against homosexuality and alcoholism remain strong" (pp. 1–2).

The heteronormative nature of society, combined with the persistent challenges faced by women to gain equal footing as men with respect to jobs, income, political might, and other types of power and privilege, creates the conditions by which lesbianism remains an identity that is transgressive and as a result can foster a sense of self-consciousness and shame, sometimes resulting in self-hatred. Barnard (2005) noted that "unlike minority groups for whom physical attributes identify their differences from the dominant culture, lesbians are a hidden population, and little is known about the scope of lesbian lifestyles" (p. 38). Lesbians are likely to be part of every type of racial, ethnic, and socioeconomic demographic and yet little research has been done on them not only because of their invisibility, but also because of the social stigma attached to being a lesbian, an additional cause of this invisibility (Barnard, 2005). Even though lesbians have become more visible, in particular, in the popular media (e.g., there are out lesbian celebrities such as Ellen DeGeneres and Jane Lynch), and there are certain states that have enacted antidiscrimination laws based upon sexual orientation, being a sexual and gender minority brings with it a set of challenges. Swim, Ferguson, and Hyers (1999) observed that the stigma of being a lesbian is a source of social pressure that inhibits behaviors associated with nontraditional gender roles, and that the fear (for lesbians or for any women) of being labeled "lesbian" is a basis of gender role socialization. Lesbians are "devalued because they are women, they are again devalued, more severely, because their existence is not dependent upon a relationship with a man" (Bobbe, 2002, p. 218). They face internalized homophobia (Anderson & Henderson, 1985; Bobbe, 2002; Ettore, 2005; Hall, 1990; Weber, 2008) and disconnection with each other (Gedro, 2006). One way that lesbians manage their stigmatized identity (Anderson & Henderson, 1985) is to employ a variety of strategies such as closeting, passing as straight, distracting, or even lying and making up fictitious "cover stories" in which they present themselves as heterosexual.

"Sexual minority women share many of the same health risks as women in the general population; however, their status as part of a stigmatized minority group is believed to increase their risk for certain health problems or health risk behaviors" (Meyer, 2003, in Bostwick, Hughes, & Johnson, 2005, p. 8). All of these factors serve to constrain their abilities to live lives that are healthy and characterized by the ability to make choices about how to establish relationships (both platonic and romantic), and how to socialize. Kerby et al. (2005) observes that research into lesbian health challenges is limited, and that not only is healthcare access restricted for lesbians (p. 46) but also that homophobic attitudes persist among healthcare professionals. Sauliner (2002) notes that lesbians experience, for example, challenges with respect to high-quality healthcare access because of long-standing provider biases, and that the negative attitudes possessed and demonstrated by providers continue to hamper the ability for lesbians to get quality healthcare. The stigma, therefore, of being a lesbian presents, in part, an explanation for higher rates of alcoholism among lesbians, and it also creates challenges for lesbians who recognize that they might have problems with alcoholism, and seek help. Even though discrimination, homophobia, heterosexism, and fear of disclosure put lesbians at increased risk for alcoholism, in the United States, lesbians "often do not feel they are receiving culturally competent care" (Dinkel, 2005, p. 10). According to Dinkel, culturally competent care consists of five constructs: (a) cultural desire, which is the genuine desire to work with culturally different groups; (b) cultural awareness, which is the act of acknowledging changes in society and in healthcare; (c) cultural knowledge, which is the process of seeking out opportunities to become educated about various world views and biological variations; (d) cultural skill, which is the ability to collect data in a sensitive way; and (e) cultural encounters, which are consistent interactions with cultural groups to extend and support the process. This cultural competence among practitioners forms part of the basis for the recommendations presented at the conclusion of this chapter, because in order to address the problem of alcoholism among lesbians, it is important for adult educators to understand the issues that are specific and unique to lesbians and to provide resources for counselors and related practitioners, to help them become culturally competent as they work with lesbian clients.

Minority Stress, Identity, and Shame. Lesbians are at heightened risk for alcoholism because of the stress associated with being a gender minority and a sexual minority. "As a result of being sexual minorities in a predominately anti-gay society, LGB individuals experience physical and emotional stress, a phenomenon that DiPlacido (1998) referred to as *minority stress*" (Weber, 2008, p. 31). Weber observed that the realization of a minority sexual identity is a factor in LGB substance abuse. Weber created an adaptation of McCarn and Fassinger's (1996) model of sexual minority identity development as a way of contextualizing the strain that sexual minorities

New Directions for Adult and Continuing Education • DOI: 10.1002/ace

(LGB) experience as they travel through the stages of identity formation. Weber noted the usefulness of understanding the stages of sexual minority identity formation developed by McCarn and Fassinger (1996) because implicit in the model is the journey that one traverses on the way to feeling whole, content, comfortable, and complete about one's sexual minority identity. The stages of this model in brief are: awareness of feeling "different," exploration of sexual feelings, deepening commitment to one's sexual identity, internalization of one's status, and finally, synthesis of one's status (Weber, 2008, p. 36). Weber offered that the model of sexual minority identity development "does underscore the emotional intensity and difficulty of the process of developing an LGB sexual identity in the context of societal oppression" (p. 44). Weber confirmed that those sexual minorities who had a substance abuse or alcohol disorder reported that they experienced more heterosexism than those who were not classified as having such a disorder. It is clear that the stress of being a sexual minority is a contributing risk factor for lesbians. It is also clear that the double stress of being a sexual minority and a gender minority presents a heightened risk for lesbians. Cabaj (2000, in Weber, 2008) "posited that substance use and abuse disconnects LGBT people from feelings of shame and anxiety, provides acceptance, fosters social comfort in bars or unfamiliar social settings, and allows for denial and even blackouts about sexual behavior" (p. 35). Additionally, the separation or ostracism that occurs for sexual minorities, including lesbians, from their families, and the difficulty in finding other lesbians for friendship or for romance, can lead to "limited social support and feelings of isolation, both of which can lead to substance abuse or mental health problems" (Green & Feinstein, 2012, p. 272). Bobbe (2002) noted that "the dynamics of unconscious shame continue to negate the lesbian child's experience of herself through dissociation of emotion, and often through self-abuse in the form of addiction" (p. 219).

Other Issues: Sexual Abuse and Depression. Hughes (2003) noted that childhood sexual abuse presents a risk factor. Rates of childhood sexual abuse were 68% for lesbians and 47% for heterosexual women. Although research has demonstrated that approximately 10–20% of women report being sexually abused in childhood, women who are in treatment for alcoholism report much higher rates, which suggests a relationship between the experience of childhood sexual abuse and alcoholism (Fleming, Mullen, Sibthorpe, Attewell, & Bammer, 1998). It has been established that childhood sexual abuse results in difficulties for victims. These difficulties include depression and substance abuse:

> Children and adolescents who experience sexual abuse are more likely to experience depression and dysthymia, borderline personality disorder, somatization disorder, substance abuse disorder, posttraumatic stress disorder, dissociative identity disorder, or bulimia nervosa; to attempt suicide; to become pregnant earlier; to engage in HIV sexual risk behaviors; to perform poorly at school; to

be arrested for sex crimes; or to commit other criminal offenses. (Friedman et al., 2011, p. 1481)

In their meta-analysis of medical and social science journals from 1980 to 2009 of studies that compared the likelihood of self-reported childhood sexual abuse, physical abuse perpetrated by parents or guardians, and peer abuse, Friedman et al. (2011) discovered that sexual minority youths were 2.9 times more likely to report childhood sexual abuse. Lesbian rates of childhood sexual abuse were 32.1%, compared with 16.9% for heterosexual females. Hyman (2009, as cited in Galvin & Brooks-Livingston, 2011, p. 17) examined the mental health of lesbians, the effect upon them of living in a heterosexist society, as well as the prevalence of child sexual abuse and the association of lifetime alcohol abuse (among sexual abuse clients) and discovered a strong correlation between these variables. In particular, Hyman discovered that there is a high prevalence of substance abuse among lesbians who have experienced child sexual abuse. Depression, a "serious mood disorder" (Barnard, 2005, p. 36) that deleteriously affects intrapersonal and interpersonal relationships, has been found to be twice as prevalent in women as men (Barnard, 2005). However, there is little research that has been conducted on depression and lesbians, who "are a unique and often hidden population within American society" (Barnard, 2005, p. 36). Bobbe (2002) noted that homophobia presents an "ongoing oppressive force" (p. 218) and that internalized homophobia can lead to depression, which can lead to drinking. However, alcohol exacerbates depression, which makes the original problem worse and can result in the downward spiral of increasing dependency (Bobbe, 2002).

Bostwick et al. (2005) similarly identified factors that co-occur and/or contribute to alcoholism in lesbians. Those factors include discrimination, homophobia, and heterosexism, leading to anxiety and depression, resulting in a higher risk for alcoholism.

Alcoholism, Alcoholics Anonymous, and Lesbian Recovered Alcoholics

There is no cure for alcoholism. It is suggested that once one has crossed the line into alcoholic drinking, abstinence is indicated. Although there are different schools of thought about this matter, again, this chapter operates with the understanding that alcoholism is a disease characterized by an inability to stop drinking once an alcoholic has begun drinking. Therefore, there are different approaches that alcoholics (and lesbian alcoholics) can take toward maintaining sobriety. Perhaps the most well-known method is Alcoholics Anonymous, which is a peer support based treatment program in which participants self-identify as alcoholics and work with others to "share their experience, strength and hope with each other so that they may solve their common problem and help others to recover from alcoholism" (Alcoholics Anonymous, 2013a, para. 1). There are multiple perspectives about the inclusiveness of Alcoholics Anonymous that bear highlighting.

Alcoholics Anonymous: Noninclusive. With respect to lesbians and Alcoholics Anonymous, it is accurate to claim that the organization was pioneered by two heterosexual, White men, Bill Wilson and Dr. Robert (Bob) Smith, and that it has its roots in religion:

> The origins of Alcoholics Anonymous can be traced to the Oxford Group, a religious movement popular in the United States and Europe in the early 20th century. Members of the Oxford Group practiced a formula of self-improvement by performing self-inventory, admitting wrongs, making amends, using prayers and meditation, and carrying the message to others. (Alcoholics Anonymous, 2013b, para. 1)

Wilke (1994) noted that Alcoholics Anonymous uses sexist language. Other criticisms of AA have included that "AA is a religion or cult with a suspiciously white, male, dominant-culture, Christian God" (Davis & Jansen, 1998, p. 172). Alcoholics Anonymous was founded by heterosexual, White men, and was based upon a Christian God; although there are meetings that are exclusively for LGBT people in recovery, criticism of AA as heterosexist, White, and patriarchal seems to persist (Matthews, Lorah, & Fenton, 2006; Pettinato, 2005; Staddon, 2005). Despite these criticisms, AA is seen as an effective method for abstinence and sobriety, and Matthews et al. (2006) suggest that gay and lesbian AA meetings are helpful.

Alcoholics Anonymous: Inclusive. There is evidence, as has been presented here, to suggest that there are lesbians who feel that Alcoholics Anonymous has a culture characterized by patriarchy and religious fundamentalism. It is important to note that although these criticisms are valid for those who offer them, and that although it has roots in the Oxford Group, Alcoholics Anonymous is not a religious organization, and it does not require religious affiliation or faith. The primary text of Alcoholics Anonymous (2008), called the "Big Book," explains its spiritual orientation (and corresponding lack of religious affiliation) by indicating the following: "When, therefore, we speak to you of God, we mean your own conception of God . . . Do not let any prejudice you may have against spiritual terms deter you from honestly asking yourself what they mean to you" (p. 47). Early in its history, Alcoholics Anonymous had a focus on helping an alcoholic, no matter what demographic, get sober. Borden (2007) described an interchange between Barry L. and Bill Wilson in which Barry asked Bill his thoughts about setting up an AA meeting for gay men, to which Bill Wilson responded that if setting up such a meeting represented the lengths to which Barry must go to help these (gay) men get sober, then it was important for Barry to do it. There are other examples that demonstrate Bill Wilson's phlegmatic orientation toward sexual minorities, but for purposes of brevity, this incident hopefully proves sufficient. Over the course of its history, Alcoholics Anonymous has included LGBT people in its

New Directions for Adult and Continuing Education • DOI: 10.1002/ace

literature, and has had LGBT meetings. In 1973, a pamphlet entitled "The Homosexual Alcoholic: A.A.'s Message of Hope to Gay Men & Women" was printed (Borden, 2007). In 1974, the General Service Conference of Alcoholics Anonymous voted to include homosexual groups in its World Directory, and in 1989, AA published a pamphlet entitled "A.A. and the Gay/Lesbian Alcoholic" (Borden, 2007). In the face of what this chapter presents as arguably conflicting points of view regarding Alcoholics Anonymous, and its appropriateness for lesbians as a means resource for achieving and maintaining sobriety, the tension produced by this conflict is important to note and presents an opportunity for further exploration.

Conclusions and Implications for Adult Educators and Related Professionals

Adult educators, particularly those in health education, have an opportunity to disrupt the particular problems that beset lesbians who are at risk for alcoholism, and lesbians who suffer from alcoholism. There are three fundamental ways that adult educators can address the issue, at three different levels. The first, through working to transform negative societal attitudes toward sexual minorities, and thus work to minimize or hopefully eliminate heterosexism, sexism, and homophobia, is admittedly a tall and ambitious order. The second is more direct, perhaps more immediate, which is to create programs for healthcare professionals to raise their awareness around lesbian identity and culture, and the particular challenges that lesbians face, and the factors that put them at risk for alcohol abuse and alcoholism. Hall (1990) noted that lesbian recovery from alcoholism is a "complex human phenomenon" (p. 109) and that there is a lack of exploration of long-term recovery in lesbian women. Weber (2008), for example, noted that sexual minorities have "special treatment concerns" in addition to recovery, such as grappling with and recovering from internalized homophobia. Weber suggested that counselor and health educators who teach and supervise mental health counselors should increase their students' awareness of the impacts of homophobia, heterosexism, and internalized homophobia on sexual minorities. With respect to lesbians and alcoholism in particular, adult educators have an opportunity to serve as agents of emancipatory change, by creating programs and services that uncover the double (or more, depending on other factors, such as race, ethnicity, religion, and disability) minority stress of being lesbian. The third way that adult educators can address the issue is to conceive, develop, and deliver programs that help lesbians successfully negotiate alcoholism, treatment, and recovery, and to, when it co-occurs as an explanatory factor, overcome the deleterious effects of homophobia and heterosexism.

Adult educators have an opportunity to serve this triply stigmatized population by providing education that raises awareness about the elevated risks for alcoholism that lesbians face. Programs that help sensitize healthcare professionals to the unique risks and needs of this population would be appropriate, so that lesbians who seek help are treated with respect, compassion, and understanding. Adult educators can work on a larger scale to create programs that work to lessen societal heterosexism and homophobia, which seem to be the fundamental underlying factor in lesbians' risk levels of alcoholism. Therefore, by addressing preventative measures, as well as the recovery measures, related to lesbians, adult educators have a unique opportunity to work for social justice through better health, wellness, and well-being for lesbians. What helps any minority helps all of society.

References

Alcoholics Anonymous. (2008). *Alcoholics Anonymous: The Big Book* (4th ed.). Retrieved from http://www.aa.org/bbonline/
Alcoholics Anonymous. (2013a). *Preamble.* Retrieved from http://www.aa.org/en_pdfs/smf-92_en.pdf
Alcoholics Anonymous. (2013b). *Origins.* Retrieved from http://www.aa.org/aatimeline/
Anderson, S., & Henderson, D. (1985). Working with lesbian alcoholics. *Social Work, 30*(6), 518–525.
Barnard, A. (2005). Effects of sexuality on lesbians' experiences of depression. *Journal of Psychosocial Nursing and Mental Health Services, 43*(10), 36–43.
Becker, K., & Walton-Moss, B. (2001). Detecting and addressing alcohol abuse in women. *Nurse Practitioner, 26*(10), 13–25.
Bobbe, J. (2002). Treatment with lesbian alcoholics: Healing shame and internalized homophobia for ongoing sobriety. *Health & Social Work, 27*(3), 218–222.
Borden, A. (2007). *The history of gay people in Alcoholics Anonymous.* Binghamton, NY: The Haworth Press.
Bostwick, W., Hughes, T., & Johnson, T. (2005). The co-occurrence of depression and alcohol dependence symptoms in a community sample of lesbians. In E. Ettore (Ed.), *Journal of Lesbian Studies: 9*(3). *Making lesbians visible in the substance abuse field* (pp. 7–18). Binghamton, NY: Harrington Park Press.
Brewer, M. (2006). The contextual factors that foster and hinder the process of recovery for alcohol dependent women. *Journal of Addictions Nursing, 17,* 175–180. doi:10.1080/10884600600862194
Cabaj, R. P. (2000). Substance abuse, internalized homophobia, and gay men and lesbians: Psychodynamic issues and clinical implications. In J. R. Guss & J. Drescher (Eds.), *Addictions in the gay and lesbian community* (pp. 5–24). Binghamton, NY: The Haworth Press.
Centers for Disease Control and Prevention (CDC). (2013). *Excessive drinking costs U.S. $223.5 billion.* Retrieved from http://www.cdc.gov/features/alcoholconsumption/
Davis, D., & Jansen, G. (1998). Making meaning of Alcoholics Anonymous for social workers: Myths, metaphors, and realities. *Social Work, 43*(2), 169–182.
Dinkel, S. (2005). Providing culturally competent care to lesbians. *Kansas Nurse, 80*(9), 10–12.
DiPlacido, J. (1998). Minority stress among lesbians, gay men, and bisexuals: A consequence of heterosexism, homophobia and stigmatization. In G. M. Herek (Ed.), *Stigma and sexual orientation: Understanding prejudice against lesbians, gays and bisexuals* (pp. 138–159). Thousand Oaks, CA: Sage.
Ettore, E. (2005). *Journal of Lesbian Studies: 9*(3). *Making lesbians visible in the substance abuse field.* Binghamton, NY: Harrington Park Press.
Faderman, L. (1991). *Odd girls and twilight lovers.* New York, NY: Penguin Books.

Fleming, J., Mullen, P. E., Sibthorpe, B., Attewell, R., & Bammer, G. (1998). The relationship between childhood sexual abuse and alcohol abuse in women—A case-control study. *Addiction*, 93(12), 1787–1798.

Friedman, M., Marshal, M., Guadamuz, T., Wei, C., Wong, C., Saewyc, E., & Stall, R. (2011). A meta-analysis of disparities in childhood sexual abuse, parental physical abuse, and peer victimization among sexual minority and sexual nonminority individuals. *American Journal of Public Health*, 101(8), 1481–1494.

Galvin, C., & Brooks-Livingston, A. (2011). Impact of remembering childhood sexual abuse on addiction recovery for young adult lesbians. *Adultspan Journal*, 10(1), 14–23.

Gedro, J. (2006, May). *Separation, subjugation, isolation and intoxication: Lesbians and fences.* Paper presented at the Adult Education Research Conference Queer Pre-Conference, Minneapolis, MN.

Gedro, J., Cervero, R., & Johnson-Bailey, J. (2004). How lesbians learn to negotiate the heterosexism of corporate America. *Human Resource Development International*, 7(2), 181–195.

Gedro, J., Mercer, F., & Iodice, J. (2012, March). Recovered alcoholics and career development: Implications for human resource development. *Human Resource Development Quarterly*, 23(1), 129–132.

Goffman, E. (1963). *Stigma: Notes on the management of spoiled identity.* New York, NY: Simon & Schuster.

Green, K., & Feinstein, B. (2012). Substance use in lesbian, gay, and bisexual populations: An update on empirical research and implications for treatment. *Psychology of Addictive Behaviors*, 26(2), 265–288.

Hall, J. (1990). Alcoholism recovery in lesbian women: A theory in development. *Scholarly Inquiry for Nursing Practice*, 4(2), 109–122.

Hasin, D., Van Rossem, R., McCloud, S., & Endicott, J. (1997). Differentiating DSM-IV alcohol dependence and abuse by course: Community heavy drinkers. *Journal of Substance Abuse*, 9, 127–135.

Hatzenbuehler, M. (2009). How does sexual minority stigma "get under the skin"? A psychological mediation framework. *Psychological Bulletin*, 135(5), 707–730.

Herbert, J., Hunt, B., & Dell, G. (1994). Counseling gay men and lesbians with alcohol problems. *Journal of Rehabilitation*, April–June, 52–57.

Hughes, T. (2003). Lesbians' drinking patterns: Beyond the data. *Substance Use & Misuse*, 38(11–13), 1739–1758.

Hughes, T. L., & Wilsnack, S. C. (1997). Use of alcohol among lesbians: Research and clinical implications. *American Journal of Orthopsychiatry*, 67(1), 20–36.

Kerby, M., Wilson, R., Nicholson, T., & White, J. (2005). Substance use and social identity in the lesbian community. In E. Ettore (Ed.), *Journal of Lesbian Studies: 9(3). Making lesbians visible in the substance use field* (pp. 45–56). Binghamton, NY: Harrington Park Press.

Matthews, C., Lorah, P., & Fenton, J. (2006). Treatment experiences of gays and lesbians in recovery from addiction: A qualitative inquiry. *Journal of Mental Health Counseling*, 28(2), 111–132.

McCarn, S., & Fassinger, R. (1996). Revisioning sexual minority identity formation: A new model of lesbian identity and its implications for counseling and research. *The Counseling Psychologist*, 24, 508–534.

Meyer, I. (2003). Prejudice, social stress, and mental health in lesbian, gay, and bisexual populations: Conceptual issues and research evidence. *Psychological Bulletin*, 129(5), 674–697.

National Institute on Alcohol Abuse and Alcoholism (NIAAA). (1995). *Diagnostic criteria for alcohol abuse and dependence.* Alcohol Alert, No. 30 PH 359. Retrieved from http://pubs.niaaa.nih.gov/publications/aa30.htm

National Institute on Alcohol Abuse and Alcoholism (NIAAA). (2000). *New Advances in Alcoholism Treatment*. Alcohol Alert, No. 49. Retrieved from http://pubs .niaaa.nih.gov/publications/aa49.htm

National Institute on Alcohol Abuse and Alcoholism (NIAAA). (2005). *Helping patients who drink too much: A clinician's guide*. Retrieved from http://pubs .niaaa.nih.gov/publications/Practitioner/CliniciansGuide2005/guide.pdf

National Institute on Alcohol Abuse and Alcoholism (NIAAA). (2013a). *Alcohol use disorders*. Retrieved from http://www.niaaa.nih.gov/alcohol-health/overview-alcohol -consumption/alcohol-use-disorders

National Institute on Alcohol Abuse and Alcoholism (NIAAA). (2013b). *Drinking statistics*. Retrieved from http://www.niaaa.nih.gov/alcohol-health/overview-alcohol -consumption/drinking-statistics

Parks, C., & Hughes, T. (2005). Alcohol use and alcohol-related problems in self-identified lesbians: An historical cohort analysis. In E. Ettore (Ed.), *Journal of Lesbian Studies: 9(3). Making lesbians visible in the substance use field* (pp. 31–44). Binghamton, NY: Harrington Park Press.

Pettinato, M. (2005). Predicting, understanding and changing: Three research paradigms regarding alcohol use among lesbians. In E. Ettore (Ed.), *Journal of Lesbian Studies: 9(3). Making lesbians visible in the substance use field* (pp. 91–101). Binghamton, NY: Harrington Park Press.

Saghir, M., & Robins, E. (1973). *Male and female homosexuality: A comprehensive investigation*. Baltimore, MD: Williams & Wilkins.

Sauliner, C. (2002). Deciding who to see: Lesbians discuss their preferences in health and mental health care providers. *Social Work, 47*(4), 355–365.

Staddon, P. (2005). Labelling out: The personal account of an ex-alcoholic lesbian feminist. In E. Ettore (Ed.), *Journal of Lesbian Studies: 9(3). Making lesbians visible in the substance use field* (pp. 69–78). Binghamton, NY: Harrington Park Press.

Swallow, J. (1983). *Out from under: Sober dykes and our friends*. San Francisco, CA: Spinsters.

Swim, J., Ferguson, M., & Hyers, L. (1999). Avoiding stigma by association: subtle prejudice against lesbians in the form of social distancing. *Basic and Applied Psychology, 21*(1), 61–68.

Weber, G. (2008). Using to numb the pain: Substance use and abuse among lesbian, gay, and bisexual individuals. *Journal of Mental Health Counseling, 30*(1), 31–48.

Wilke, D. (1994). Women and alcoholism: How male-as-norm bias affects research, assessment and treatment. *Health & Social Work, 19*(1), 29–35.

JULIE GEDRO is an associate professor of business, management, and economics at Empire State College/State University of New York.

6

This chapter addresses tobacco use among sexual minorities. It examines research on the prevalence of tobacco use in the lesbian, gay, bisexual, and transgender (LGBT) community and discusses why tobacco use within this group continues to significantly exceed that of the general population.

Tobacco Use Among Sexual Minorities

Lawrence O. Bryant, Lorenzo Bowman

This chapter addresses tobacco use among sexual minorities. We will examine research on the prevalence of tobacco use in the lesbian, gay, bisexual, and transgender (LGBT) community and discuss why tobacco use within this group continues to significantly exceed that of the general population. The problem presents opportunities for adult educators to examine the ways LGBT learn to smoke, identify reasons for the disproportionately high prevalence, and develop nicotine addiction interventions that are culturally relevant and efficacious.

Tobacco addiction continues to be the leading preventable cause of sickness and death worldwide and in the United States (CDC, 2013; WHO, 2013). Although there has been a consistent decrease in tobacco use in the United States since the 1960s, 20% of adults still smoke (CDC, 2013). Tobacco use is especially common among sexual minorities. The overall prevalence of tobacco use in LGBT populations is unknown due to the limitations of nonrandom samples and small samples of particular groups (i.e., transgender). Nevertheless, almost all studies that have specifically included the LGBT population indicate that LGBT individuals smoke at higher rates and face greater potential for health disparities than the general public (ACS, 2011; ALA, 2010; Clarke & Coughlin, 2012).

Rates of smoking among LGBT youth range from 38% to 59% (Ryan, Wortley, Easton, Pederson, & Greenwood, 2001), compared to a prevalence rate among the total youth population ranging from 28% to 35% (Rosario & Schrimshaw, 2010). Some studies have found that adult LGBT smoking rates ranged as high as 50%, compared to 28% among heterosexual adults in the United States (Clarke & Coughlin, 2012; Smith, Thomson, Offen, & Malone, 2008). In addition, results from the largest survey of transgender people in the United States indicated that smoking rates were 30% higher in the transgender population than in the general U.S. population (Grant et al., 2011).

NEW DIRECTIONS FOR ADULT AND CONTINUING EDUCATION, no. 142, Summer 2014 © 2014 Wiley Periodicals, Inc.
Published online in Wiley Online Library (wileyonlinelibrary.com) • DOI: 10.1002/ace.20095

When individuals become addicted to tobacco products, they put themselves at risk for many serious diseases including lung cancer, Chronic Obstructive Lung Disease (COPD), emphysema, asthma, cardiovascular disease, chronic bronchitis, coronary artery disease, and oral cancers (CDC, 2013). This risk exposure is a significant health and wellness issue that needs to be addressed in sexual minority communities. Additionally, larger social issues such as homophobia, racism, and discrimination intersect with this health risk to present a formidable challenge for the LGBT community. Here, adult educators can provide expertise and guidance in helping address some of these challenging social issues

Why Should Adult Educators Be Concerned About Smoking in the LGBT Community?

Since learning is central to health, adult educators possess the knowledge, skills, and abilities to increase awareness of the negative health effects of smoking on the body (Hill, 2011). In addition, adult education's social justice commitment demands accountability by the tobacco companies regarding their unscrupulous marketing practices targeting the LGBT community. This targeted marketing has been extensively addressed in the literature. Drabble (2008) noted that the LGBT community and HIV/AIDS organizations have increasingly been targeted for "*specialized*" marketing. He suggested that this may contribute to the increased smoking prevalence in this community and that prompt attention was warranted to this practice. This targeting is done through four primary methods: (a) sponsorship, (b) fundraising, (c) advertising, and (d) promotions (Drabble, 2008).

A report by the American Lung Association (2010) suggests that attention should be given to smoking in the LGBT community for the following reasons:

- The high prevalence of smoking among sexual minorities is associated with increased morbidity and mortality.
- Tobacco companies' contempt for the LGBT community and strategic marketing toward this population make this a social justice issue.
- There is a lack of governmental resources allocated for cessation and prevention within this group.
- Health concerns and employee health insurance companies often prompt individuals to learn behaviors that promote healthier lifestyle choices.
- Strategies such as community-based participatory research (CBPR) allow LGBT to engage in solutions that help address this formidable challenge to the health and wellness of their community.

"We also need fresh approaches and new allies [in the war on tobacco]" (ALA, 2010, p. 17). This robust call for action puts adult educators in a unique position to develop cessation programs and advocate for clean air policies that address the special needs of the LGBT community. Adult education's staunch

New Directions for Adult and Continuing Education • DOI: 10.1002/ace

commitment to social justice and social action provides the impetus to galvanize the LGBT community to take action against tobacco companies and bar owners that place profit and financial gain above the health of the LGBT community.

In addition, adult educators have a proven track record in areas such as program planning, social learning, CBPR, and curriculum development. These skills provide an opportunity to develop tobacco control programs with an emphasis on prevention, resource allocation, and policy change. According to the ALA (2010), these types of comprehensive tobacco control programs are extremely effective:

> Campaigns that work to counter the advertising assault of the tobacco industry have been shown to successfully prevent the general population, especially youth, from smoking. Such media campaigns have educated the public about the deceptive marketing tactics of the tobacco industry. This, in turn has resulted in an increased negative view of tobacco companies, stronger anti-tobacco attitudes, and lower rates of smoking. There is evidence that similar efforts, specifically tailored for the LGBT community, would be effective. (p. 15)

Finally, adult educators can play a huge role in engaging the LGBT community in CBPR. This engaging process can help lay the groundwork for tobacco-related advocacy and the promotion of policy change at local and state levels. Stakeholders in the community can identify and make connections with advocates working in tobacco prevention. This process also serves as an opportunity to raise awareness of tobacco use as an LGBT health issue and to increase community buy-in for future policy efforts.

Adult educators can also contribute to effective smoking cessation interventions by designing and facilitating research projects that directly impact the LGBT community. In addition, they can help facilitate and work with LGBT communities to offer solutions and promote smoking cessations projects that address the many reasons for the high smoking rates among this population.

Why Are Smoking Rates Higher in the LGBT Community?

There are multiple reasons for higher rates among LGBT; chief among these is gay social spaces. One of the central places where gay nightlife unfolds is in bars. The bar culture plays a large role in tobacco use among LGBT people (Bryant, Bowman, & Damarin, 2011). These men and women often report feeling socially marginalized, and, therefore, they congregate among colleagues, friends, and acquaintances who are more accepting of their sexual orientation and lifestyle. It is at these venues that tobacco companies target the LGBT community in terms of strategic marketing. They are in harm's way since most of the places where this population congregates are smoke filled and support smoking behavior. These factors along with tobacco companies' targeted marketing make LGBT communities increasingly susceptible to higher smoking rates than the general population.

New Directions for Adult and Continuing Education • DOI: 10.1002/ace

Tobacco Industry Marketing

Because of mainstream media stigmatization, sexual minority populations may be more susceptible to targeted tobacco industry marketing (Eliason, Dibble, Gordon, & Soliz, 2012). Although mainstream advertisers mostly ignore the LGBT community in their marketing campaigns, the tobacco companies have the dubious distinction of being one of the first to develop advertisements and marketing materials that specifically target the LGBT community (ALA, 2010). Moreover, gay and lesbian populations report more exposure to tobacco advertising than their heterosexual counterparts (Diley, Spigner, Boysun, Dent, & Pizacani, 2008). According to Drabble (2008), the tobacco industry targets the LGBT community through the methods mentioned earlier (sponsorship, fundraising, advertising, and promotions). One infamous tobacco industry campaign provides a good example of how the industry targets the LGBT market. Between 1995 and 1997, R. J. Reynolds engaged in a crusade called "Project SCUM" which stands for "Subculture Urban Marketing." Reynolds tried to market Camel and Red Kamel cigarettes to San Francisco area "consumer subcultures" of "alternative life styles." Reynolds targeted gay and homeless people in the Castro district in San Francisco, where the company noted, "The opportunity exists for a cigarette manufacturer to dominate" (Washington, 2002, p. 1093). In addition, the targets were described as "rebellious, Generation X-ers" and "street people." A retrospective study investigating the health and well-being of a national sample of LGBT found increased drug use among participants in states, such as California, where discriminatory policies such as banning same-sex marriage are in place (Hatzenbuehler, McLaughlin, Keyes, & Hasin, 2010). In taking advantage of these social problems, Project SCUM organizers planned to exploit the high rates of drug use in the "*subculture*" target group by saturating nontraditional retail outlets with the Camel brand. In one copy of the plan, "the word 'scum' was crossed out and the word 'Sourdough' substituted by a cautious executive. After such careful sanitizing the final document emerged as Project Sourdough with no clear written evidence that young LGBT participants had been targeted" (Washington, 2002, p. 1093). Paradoxically, it was through the state of California's litigation (Tobacco Settlement Agreement) with the tobacco industry that documents related to this ruthless campaign came to light; during these proceedings, it became very apparent how the tobacco companies targeted and benefited financially from the LGBT community, while at the same time vilifying them. In spite of these egregious practices by the tobacco industry, some organizations are beginning to fight back at the national and local levels.

Prevention and Awareness Campaigns

To combat these efforts by tobacco companies, national organizations are beginning to raise awareness and galvanize their resources to fight against campaigns like this. The American Lung Association recently created a landmark

New Directions for Adult and Continuing Education • DOI: 10.1002/ace

report titled "Smoking Out a Deadly Threat" providing a variety of historical and recent data on the smoking disparities affecting the gay community (ALA, 2010). The ALA noted the aggressive nature of tobacco industry marketing in perpetuating high smoking rates in the LGBT community. They further noted the invisibility of the transgender community in population-based surveys. Recommendations for addressing this disparity include policies that reduce tobacco use in all populations, including increased cigarette and other tobacco product taxes, targeted awareness programs, and educating the public about the deceptive marketing practices of tobacco companies. According to the ALA, culturally competent stop smoking services to the LGBT community are also important. They include the following:

- Recruiting LGBT friendly facilitators with prior experience leading support groups.
- Finding a welcoming and easily accessible place that is gay friendly to host cessation activities.
- Providing culturally competent cessation programs within the confines of a comprehensive tobacco control program for the LGBT population.
- Certification by a recognized agency or program such as the ALA.
- When possible, making educational materials appropriate for LGBT populations.
- Culturally competent staff should be trained to assure safety and confidentiality for LGBT participants.

The American Cancer Society (ACS) has placed a similar call to action to promote tobacco-free spaces in the LGBT community. They propose increasing taxes on tobacco, making LGBT spaces tobacco free, and encouraging smokers to join their "Action Network" in promoting smoking cessation. One example of this call to action is through promoting participation in the "Gay American Smoke Out" which coincides with the "Great American Smoke Out" sponsored yearly during the month of November by the ACS. Participants are encouraged to go at least 24 hours without smoking. Given adult educator's skills in creating education programs and providing a platform for social action, they should also be on the front lines in efforts to promote effective smoking cessation strategies.

Recently, the authors have expanded on the above recommendations by conducting a comprehensive needs assessment program investigating tobacco use in the LGBT community in the Atlanta Georgia metro area. Both quantitative and qualitative data were collected for this study. Four focus groups were conducted with LGBT former smokers, nonsmokers, and smokers to determine tobacco-related knowledge, attitudes, and behaviors, and reasons LGBT community members initiate and continue tobacco use. In addition, survey data were collected from 685 individuals at six local LGBT events and organizations to determine the importance of smoking as a health issue in the LGBT community. Health behaviors such as smoking, exercise habits, body mass index, knowledge and opinions on smoking policies, and the acceptance of to-bacco funding in the LGBT community were obtained. The authors concluded that tobacco use is significantly higher in the LGBT community in Atlanta than in the general population. The authors also found that the local gay commu-nity had been strategically targeted by tobacco companies. Interestingly, the authors also discovered that the LGBT community is unaware of these serious health disparities (Bryant et al., 2011). Furthermore, almost all LGBT individ-uals who smoked reported doing so in order to manage high levels of daily stress. Thus, for these individuals, the stress of societal stigma, homophobia, prejudice, and discrimination almost certainly contributes to smoking patterns (Bryant & Bowman, 2011; NALGBTCC, 2003).

Smoking Cessation Strategies

During the early 1980s, the AIDS epidemic propelled the gay community into a type of social activism and organizing rarely seen in any popula-tion. The effort was primarily led by gay men and lesbians, both White and African American, in groups such as ACT-UP and the National Associ-ation of Black and White Men Together (NABWMT; Landers, Pickett, Ren-nie, & Wakefield, 2011). Additionally, these organizations promoted activities that were dedicated to challenging racism, discrimination, homophobia, and HIV/AIDS.

Currently, some LGBT-focused organizations have established antismok-ing campaigns designed to reach LGBT people, for example, "Cigarettes Are My Greatest Enemy." This project was a multifaceted, LGBT focused, media campaign designed to attract and engage the LGBT community through palm cards, flyers, billboards, print ads, postcards, and transit ads. This project was funded by the American Legacy Foundation (Cigarettes Are My Greatest En-emy, n.d.).

The American Legacy Foundation (ALF) is the first national philanthropy organization to identify the gay, lesbian, bisexual, and transgender commu-nity as a priority group for countering the tobacco industry's marketing efforts (ALF, 2013). This organization has worked tirelessly to counter the tobacco in-dustry's marketing efforts. The foundation shows LGBT community represen-tatives ways in which the tobacco industry has strategically marketed to them while simultaneously holding the community up to scorn and ridicule (Bryant et al., 2011). Another LGBT-focused smoking cessation programs called "The Last Drag" highlights awareness campaigns to draw attention to the ways the tobacco industry has purposely targeted LGBT communities. According to Eliason et al. (2012), "The Last Drag provides a safe space for LGBT smok-ers to go through the quitting process in a supportive group environment" (p. 868). A 2007 report on this program in San Francisco boast impressive successes, ranging from 65 to 92% at class ending, 53 to 83% at one month, 36 to 63% at 3 months, and 36 to 65% at the end of 6 months. These data highlight the value of cessation programs that are culturally tailored toward the needs of the LGBT community (Eliason et al., 2012).

Other groups such as the National Black Gay Men's Advocacy Coalition (NBGMAC) are important community mobilization forces in dealing with Black gay and bisexual men's health issues. This mobilization is an example of how a marginalized community can come together and respond to changing health needs (Landers et al., 2011). These needs go beyond just HIV/AIDS and include health disparities such as are seen in nicotine addiction.

Adult educators can serve as avenues of social change for underserved populations such as sexual minority communities by developing projects and facilitating research in concert with the LGBT community.

Adult Education Smoking Cessation Projects

The above-mentioned study conducted in Atlanta suggests that members of the LGBT community have their own ideas about smoking cessation strategies that may be effective for their community. These ideas present opportunities for adult educators to develop more effective interventions. For example, a recent community meeting held in Atlanta identified strategies that may be effective in addressing nicotine addiction (Bryant & Bowman, 2010). These strategies included the following:

- Providing LGBT-specific cessation programs.
- Raising awareness about the LGBT smoking disparity to help mobilize the community.
- Identifying LGBT spokespersons to advocate against smoking.
- Promoting health and wellness programs for the LGBT community.
- Connecting smoking to social justice issues.

LGBT members feel that any campaign should include hard-to-reach groups, for example, youth, low-income, and transgendered individuals. Additionally, such campaigns should make a clear case for why cessation matters to LGBT people. The role of smoke-filled LGBT venues in fostering addiction should be addressed in advocacy for clean air laws. Current and former smokers often claimed that they began the habit when they "came out" and started frequenting LGBT bars where smoking was considered normal (Bryant et al., 2011). Some LGBT members have suggested convincing bars to consider smoke-free policies, such as getting community organizations to choose smoke-free venues for their fundraisers and giving the bars financial incentives.

The above issues should encourage adult educators to develop effective educational interventions that deter the initiation of smoking as well as develop targeted smoking cessation programs designed to raise awareness about the tobacco problem. In addition, the American Lung Association suggests the research community should evaluate promising innovations and interventions that prevent tobacco use and promote health and wellness in sexual minority communities.

The ACS (2011) emphasizes the value of "quit[ting] smoking today." They note the immediate and long-term benefits of quitting. For example, after 20 minutes of not smoking, blood pressure drops to a level close to that before an individual's last cigarette and the temperature in the hands and feet return to normal. Moreover, after 8 hours, carbon monoxide levels in the blood return to normal; at 24 hours, the probability of a heart attack decreases; after a few months of not smoking, circulation improves and lung function increases up to 30%. After 1 year, the probability of having a heart attack is cut in half. These health-related factors make it imperative for adult educators to promote programs that increase awareness about the benefits of quitting and decreasing tobacco usage. In a larger adult education context, these tobacco control efforts could be couched in research that includes elements of social justice and social learning theories. Additionally, other factors that impact smoking cessation, such as alcohol and drug use, should be explored. Finally, adult educators should reach out to LGBT community leaders, members, and entertainment figures to help increase awareness about the dangers of tobacco use to the health and welfare of sexual minority communities.

Conclusion

Historically, members of different segments of society have marginalized LGBT persons. In national efforts to educate all Americans about the dangers of tobacco use and smoking in particular, the LGBT community has been overlooked. Indeed, the literature indicates that the tobacco companies have targeted LGBT communities across the country. However, little has been done to customize smoking cessation programs for the LGBT community. Adult education programs are an ideal vessel for helping to raise awareness about smoking disparities in the LGBT community. In the wake of a national outcry by the American Lung Association, calling to action educators, public health personnel, and community organizations, adult educators should be in the lead. Indeed, the data indicate that the tobacco companies have targeted LGBT communities across the country with great determination and persistence. However, adult educators possess the necessary qualifications and knowledge to lead the charge in developing effective cessation programs and to advocate for change in keeping with its social justice tradition.

References

American Cancer Society (ACS). (2011). *Tobacco and GLBT community*. Retrieved from http://www.glbthealth.org/documents/GLBTTobacco.pdf

American Legacy Foundation (ALF). (2013). *American legacy foundation pulls back the "orange curtain" on Project SCUM.* Retrieved from http://www.legacyforhealth.org/newsroom/press-releases/american-legacy-foundation-pulls-back-the-orange-curtain-on-project-scum

American Lung Association (ALA). (2010). *Smoking out a deadly threat: Tobacco use in the LGBT community.* New York, NY: Author.

Bryant, L., & Bowman, L. (2010, June). *Black gay men at midlife: Learning self-acceptance.* Paper presented at the 2010 Adult Education Research Conference (AERC), Sacramento, California.

Bryant, L., & Bowman, L. (2011, June). *Using emancipatory transformative learning to address smoking behavior in the LGBT community: A quantitative study.* Paper presented at the 2011 Adult Education Research Conference (AERC), Ontario, Canada.

Bryant, L., Bowman, L., & Damarin, A. (2011). Assessment for a better understanding of tobacco use by LGBT Atlantans. *Respiratory Care Education Annual, 20,* 63–73.

Centers for Disease Control and Prevention (CDC). (2013). *Smoking and tobacco use; information by topic; adult data.* Retrieved from http://www.cdc.gov/tobacco/data_statistics/by_topic/adult_data/

Cigarettes Are My Greatest Enemy. (n.d.). Retrieved from http://www.lgbttobacco.org/files/GREATEST_ENEMY.pdf

Clarke, M. P., & Coughlin, J. R. (2012). Prevalence of smoking among the lesbian, gay, bisexual, transsexual, transgender and queer (LGBTTQ) subpopulations in Toronto—The Toronto Rainbow Tobacco Survey (TRTS). *Canadian Journal of Public Health, 103*(2), 132–136.

Diley, J. A., Spigner, C., Boysun, M. J., Dent, C. W., & Pizacani, B. A. (2008). Does tobacco industry marketing excessively impact lesbian, gay and bisexual communities? *Tobacco Control, 17*(6), 385–390.

Drabble, L. (2008). Alcohol, tobacco, and pharmaceutical industry funding: Considerations for organizations serving lesbian, gay, bisexual, and transgender communities. *Journal of Gay & Lesbian Social Services, 11*(1), 1–26.

Eliason, M., Dibble, S., Gordon, R., & Soliz, G. (2012). The Last Drag: An evaluation of an LGBT-specific smoking intervention. *Journal of Homosexuality, 59*(6), 864–869.

Grant, J. M., Mottet, L., Tanis, J. E., Harrison, J., Herman, J., & Keisling, M. (2011). *Injustice at every turn: A report of the national transgender discrimination survey.* National Center for Transgender Equality. Retrieved from http://www.thetaskforce.org/reports_and_research/ntds

Hatzenbuehler, L., McLaughlin, K., Keyes, M., & Hasin, D. (2010). The impact of institutional discrimination on psychiatric disorders in lesbian, gay, and bisexual populations: A prospective study. *American Journal of Public Health, 100,* 452–459.

Hill, L. H. (2011). Health education as an arena for adult educators' engagement in social justice. In L. H. Hill (Ed.), *New Directions for Adult and Continuing Education: No. 130. Adult education for health and wellness* (pp. 99–104). San Francisco, CA: Jossey-Bass.

Landers, S., Pickett, J., Rennie, L., & Wakefield, S. (2011). Community perspectives on developing a sexual health agenda for gay and bisexual men. *AIDS and Behavior, 15*(1), 101–106.

National Association of Lesbian, Gay, Bisexual and Transgender Community Centers (NALGBTCC). (2003). *Tobacco control program final report.* Garden Grove, CA: Author.

Rosario, M., & Schrimshaw, E. (2010). Cigarette smoking as a coping strategy: Negative implications for subsequent psychological distress among lesbian, gay, and bisexual youths. *Journal of Pediatric Psychology, 36,* 1–12.

Ryan, H., Wortley, P. M., Easton, A., Pederson, L., & Greenwood, G. (2001). Smoking among lesbians, gays, and bisexuals: A review of the literature. *American Journal of Preventive Medicine, 21*(2), 142–149.

Smith, E. A., Thomson, K., Offen, N., & Malone, R. E. (2008). "If you know you exist, it's just marketing poison": Meanings of tobacco industry targeting in the lesbian, gay, bisexual, and transgender community. *American Journal of Public Health*, 98(6), 996–1003.

Washington, H. A. (2002). Burning love: Big tobacco takes aim at LGBT youths. *American Journal of Public Health*, 92(7), 1086–1095.

World Health Organization (WHO). (2013). *Report on the global tobacco epidemic, 2008.* Retrieved from http://who.int/tobacco/mpower/gtcr_download/en/

LAWRENCE O. BRYANT *is an assistant professor at Georgia State University, Byrdine Lewis School of Nursing and Health Profession, Department of Respiratory Therapy.*

LORENZO BOWMAN *is a professor of business and management at DeVry University/Keller Graduate School of Management, Atlanta, Georgia, and is a member of the State Bar of Georgia.*

New Directions for Adult and Continuing Education • DOI: 10.1002/ace

7

This chapter explores the factors that contribute to the disclosure and communication experiences of HIV-negative gay men with one or more autoimmune diseases.

HIV-Negative Gay Men and Autoimmune Diseases

Joshua C. Collins, Tonette S. Rocco

An estimated 50 million Americans have been diagnosed with autoimmune diseases (American Autoimmune Related Diseases Association, n.d.-a), which can include commonly known chronic illnesses, such as Crohn's disease, ulcerative colitis, lupus, celiac disease, and rheumatoid arthritis (American Autoimmune Related Diseases Association, n.d.-b). The fields of medicine and public health have historically struggled to strictly define and categorize autoimmune disorders (ADs) because of the broad range of health issues that may be classified as such (Delaleu & Peck, 2009), but generally, ADs are "specific, adapted immune reactions against specific self antigens" (Serefhanoglu, Tapan, Ertenli, Kalyoncu, & Uner, 2010, p. 826), meaning that an individual's immune system may sometimes attack perfectly healthy body cells and tissue by mistake. Very often, the onset of an AD may be triggered by considerable stress (O'Leary, 1990), such as dealing with the loss of a partner, remaining in the closet, coming out as gay and dealing with the aftermath, or experiencing a long period of unemployment. Likewise, continued struggles with ADs may often be traced in parallel with times of stress in the patient's life (Kung, 1995). And while treatments do exist to ease the symptoms of most ADs, these illnesses are often distinguished within the medical community as having no known cures (Cohen, 2004), making dealing with outbreaks and relapses extremely stressful.

Gay men are often automatically associated with HIV and/or AIDS, and other health concerns—such as non-HIV autoimmune diseases—are considered secondary for gay men, both outside and within communities of sexual minorities (Jowett & Peel, 2009; Lipton, 2004). A simple Google search for "HIV-negative gay men" returns over 150,000 hits primarily related to their potential or risk for becoming infected. The same is true for the over 1,500 results in Google Scholar. However, the health concerns of gay men can be just as diverse (and maybe even more diverse) as those experienced by

NEW DIRECTIONS FOR ADULT AND CONTINUING EDUCATION, no. 142, Summer 2014 © 2014 Wiley Periodicals, Inc.
Published online in Wiley Online Library (wileyonlinelibrary.com) • DOI: 10.1002/ace.20096

heterosexual people and can be, in part, related to the stress of being a sexual minority in contexts that do not protect their civil and human rights nor value their unique contributions to society. These concerns may even be dismissed as frivolous or immoral. Coming out or choosing not to come out to family, friends, and at work are all difficult and complex situations that can contribute to the overall health of gay men (Meyer, 1995). For example, of the challenges faced by sexual minorities, as many as 40% of homeless youth are sexual minorities (Williams Institute, 2012), forced to leave their homes because of who they are. Homophobia (fear of or dislike for gay men and lesbians) and heterosexism (intentional or unintentional exclusion of sexual minorities) contribute to a sociopolitical culture that stigmatizes gay identity and makes it difficult for many to overcome ignorance and stereotypes, to come out, and/or to deal with unexpected life events such as illness effectively (Burn, Kadlec, & Rexer, 2005).

This chapter explores the factors that contribute to the disclosure and communication experiences of HIV-negative gay men with one or more autoimmune diseases. As the majority of literature on gay men and chronic illness, including autoimmune disease (AD), has focused on positive HIV status (Lipton, 2004), this chapter aims to elucidate concerns for a group of gay men often overlooked.

The Issue: Gay Identity, HIV-Negative Status, and Autoimmune Diseases

Many gay men and lesbians say that they have known their sexual orientation, or that they were different, since childhood or teenage years (Calzo, Antonucci, Mays, & Cochran, 2011). Others claim to have discovered their sexuality in adulthood or to have a more "fluid" sense of sexuality allowing for the development of same-sex attraction over the course of time (Vrangalova & Savin-Williams, 2012). Regardless of when gay identity is realized, most experience some level of personal and interpersonal struggle in understanding and internalizing their sexual orientation (Adams, 2011). In this way, the sexual identity of gay men and lesbians is differentiated from that of heterosexuals who understand and are accepted not only for, but often regardless of, their sexuality. Because of this, gay men and lesbians often seek refuge in the company of one another in order to feel less isolated as a sexual minority (Hutson, 2010; e.g., pride networks, support groups, etc.). Most gay identity development theories recognize this interaction as a crucial component to a fully integrated gay identity (Plummer, 2013). However, even within communities of other sexual minorities, gay men often find ways to separate and further divide themselves into smaller, more exclusive social groups (Isay, 2009). One common division in communities of gay men is along lines of known HIV status (Smit et al., 2012).

Autoimmune diseases may be prevalent in gay men or other groups that experience identity-based stress (Lipton, 2004). Because stigma exists to propel assumptions that identity as gay—when coupled with an AD—usually denotes one's status as HIV-positive (Jowett & Peel, 2009; Lipton, 2004), we note from personal experience that many gay men are not comfortable asking their doctors certain questions or disclosing certain information to others, even if they generally feel comfortable in their relationship with that person. This sentiment has been reflected in recent research, with one gay male participant in Adams, McCreanor, and Braun's (2013) study reflecting:

> I know that my doctor is not altogether up to date with things that might affect gay men more than they might affect straight men and their families, and so that's why I go to a different doctor for gay stuff, but I wouldn't say that he discriminates. (p. 893)

We also note that sexual minorities' experiences with ADs may be unique in that the stress related to the illness is inseparable from who they are (Jowett & Peel, 2009), further mystifying the questioning and disclosure process. Stress has been linked to identity as a sexual minority (Lewis, Derlega, Griffin, & Krowinski, 2003) and identity as a sexual minority to various risk factors for health and wellness concerns, including breast cancer (Dibble, Roberts, & Nussey, 2004), heart disease (Harcourt, 2006), and alcoholism (Greenwood & Gruskin, 2007). Stress related to being a sexual minority is also linked to willingness to seek medical advice and attention for certain stigmatized conditions such as autoimmune diseases (Lipton, 2004). Some sexual minorities have expressed the feeling that their chronic illnesses are explicitly and irreconcilably connected to sexuality (Jowett & Peel, 2009).

Some research indicates that sexual minorities with chronic illnesses may become isolated from other sexual minorities (Wilton, 1997). Indeed, among gay men HIV has so long been the dominant focus of healthcare concerns and conversations that the community pushes other problems to the margins (Lipton, 2004). Additionally, gay men's disproportionate focus on HIV may contribute to the stereotype of gay men as insatiably sexual, diverting attention away from other incredibly relevant health and wellness concerns such as ADs (Jowett & Peel, 2009). Though HIV-negative, the first author of this chapter has experienced marginalizing assumptions when revealing his own AD, Mucha–Habermann disease, which affects the skin, bringing to surface irritating, red lesions. On more than one occasion, friends, mentors, coworkers, and even doctors have presumed to know his HIV status simply in being aware of his sexual orientation (gay), his struggles with Mucha–Habermann, or seeing these red lesions. These experiences likely stem from the stereotypical view of gay men as self-damaging and "sick" (Adams et al., 2013). Thus, men who are gay and HIV-negative may also develop and assert their identities and health by distancing themselves from HIV or by being clear about their status as negative to avoid or defer stigma (Lipton, 2004; Smit et al., 2012). The following sections will discuss issues related to assumptions, exclusion, and dismissal of HIV-negative gay men with autoimmune diseases.

Assumptions. In the gay community and in society at large, there remains great stigma directed at HIV-positive gay men (Smit et al., 2012). HIV-negative gay men are often apprehensive to date those who are positive. Some may also be fearful of being associated with HIV in certain settings (i.e., perhaps their family is uneducated about HIV, gay identity, or both) simply by nature of their sexual orientation. When gay men reveal to others, including some medical professionals, that they have an AD, assumptions are sometimes made regarding their HIV status (Lipton, 2004). Additionally, gay men often "[stigmatize] those with chronic illness because of a culture that emphasizes bodily perfection, idealizing 'slim', 'fit' and abled bodies" (Jowett & Peel, 2009, p. 462). Because of this, HIV-negative gay men with ADs may choose to be clear about their negative HIV status early on in romantic relationships, with healthcare professionals, and at school and work (Lipton, 2004) in order to avoid any additional stigma. They may avoid romantic relationships with HIV-positive men in order to avoid assumptions about their own status that could result from having a partner who is open with most or all people about being HIV-positive. As Lipton (2004) noted:

> For a gay man who is ill, the stigma surrounding a homosexual orientation is compounded not only by the cultural stigma ascribed to all diseases, but also by the unique shadow of AIDS-related stigma that the legacy of HIV casts on a gay man who is living with any illness nowadays. (p. 9)

In the case of the first author of this chapter, for example, the red lesions sometimes caused by his Mucha–Habermann disease have been mistaken by some as being similar to the lesions experienced by some HIV/AIDS patients. A gay man in a similar situation may choose to avoid HIV-positive partners whose association may increase the likelihood others, including healthcare professionals or coworkers and colleagues, will perceive he is also positive. Sometimes when revealing an AD, which can be indicative of many issues and problems with the immune system, doctors may assume to know the HIV status of a patient (Lipton, 2004). Additionally, both HIV-negative and HIV-positive gay men with ADs that could potentially affect sexual health or activity may be hesitant to communicate about their struggles. They may shy away from discussing the realities of the relationship between an AD and their sex lives—at least with health service providers with whom they are not comfortable also disclosing their sexual orientation (Adams et al., 2013).

Furthermore, HIV-negative gay men who have ADs which may require them to go to the doctor's office frequently may develop and engage strategies for distancing themselves from and coping with their illness (Jowett & Peel, 2009). Often these strategies may involve simply disclosing the actual problem (the AD) and making negative HIV status clear, but in cases when the disclosure of the AD itself may cause stigmatization, different paths are taken. Other strategies might include insistent social distance from HIV-positive people or charitable events within the gay community, silence or avoiding the topic or

New Directions for Adult and Continuing Education • DOI: 10.1002/ace

questions when they arise, or fabricating alternative reasons for frequent doctor's visits, regular medication, or numerous periods of illness.

Exclusion. Non-HIV illnesses are often seen as secondary concerns within the gay community, where fundraising and awareness regarding HIV has been a prominent concern since the 1980s (Adams et al., 2013; Jowett & Peel, 2009; Lipton, 2004). HIV-negative gay men with ADs may become excluded from beneficial adult health education services because they are not HIV-positive, though it is possible they experience similar immune and other health issues. Exclusion may become a stressor or even contribute to depression that can often exacerbate the experience with the AD (Lewis et al., 2003). Because, for the most part, the gay community deems concerns related to HIV as more important than concerns related to ADs or other health conditions, HIV-negative gay men who suffer continual AD discomfort in part because of gay identity-based stressors, such as deciding when, to whom, and how much to disclose to others, may themselves feel marginalized or less important because their health concerns are not discussed. For very serious autoimmune diseases, the experience of disclosure could be similar to that of disclosing HIV status and could bring to the surface, especially among romantic partners, fears or distrust related to presumed HIV status or concerns related directly to the AD, such as being more susceptible to other illnesses. A new romantic relationship may bring about many additional stressors that could trigger reactions and AD flare-ups. The partner with the AD might feel that keeping it a secret would diminish trust in the relationship, particularly if it is something that will be recurring frequently or cause a sudden and inexplicable illness. In these instances, it is logical to think that HIV-negative gay men with ADs must integrate the condition into their identity even if that is an uncomfortable experience, but the process of integration is often slow and difficult (Lipton, 2004). As with HIV-positive gay men, an HIV-negative gay man's disclosure of AD can be like a second coming out depending on how severe the condition.

Dismissal. While many might assume that health service providers such as doctors, nurses, and physician assistants would generally be both professional and knowledgeable enough to circumvent and disregard stereotypes about gay men and health, the fact remains that in healthcare professions, "homophobia is still an ever present reality" (Jowett & Peel, 2009, p. 467). One of Jowett and Peel's (2009) gay male participants with an AD even stated that his doctor "felt entitled to pronounce judgmentally about [his] lifestyle at a point when [he was] feeling physically unwell and, therefore, vulnerable" (p. 467). For this reason, many gay men, including those with ADs, feel more comfortable with doctors who are also sexual minorities.

Certain ADs are sometimes assumed to be related to or indicative of positive HIV status or other diseases in gay men, even among medical professionals (Jowett & Peel, 2009). However, to assume that the presence of any particular AD is likely related to a patient's HIV status, either positive or negative, is dismissive. These kinds of dismissive assumptions place the burden of communication regarding the AD and HIV status solely on gay patients, which may prove uncomfortable. Dismissal of HIV-negative gay men's struggles with ADs is not confined to experiences with healthcare professionals. Dismissal may also occur among other gay men who do not associate continued struggles with ADs necessarily with being gay in any way. HIV-negative gay men may be dismissed out of hand by friends who think that because the AD is not "killing" them, they should not be complaining. This kind of dismissal is characteristic of many gay men's perceptions that issues associated with HIV/AIDS are not only the most prevalent within their community but also the most important.

Implications for Adult and Community Health Educators

Lipton (2004) offered six guidelines for addressing concerns of gay men with non-HIV chronic illnesses: recognizing the legacy of pathology, promoting empowerment, group work with gay men living with non-HIV chronic illnesses, responding to ethnocultural diversity, addressing aging, and advocating for change. Expanding on these guidelines, we offer a number of implications for adult education broadly and two specific types of adult educators, healthcare providers and patient educators.

Adult education should provide mechanisms for empowering all gay men, not just programming for HIV-positive people. Sessions and Cervero (2001) describe the politics and power inherent in the gay community—"the club" whose members are HIV-positive and hold positions of power and authority in most of the adult education outreach work done in the gay community. This creates a disempowering climate for HIV-negative people, especially those with other health concerns. There is more to this community than just HIV status. The health concerns and adult education needs in the gay community run along the same lines as in any other community. We need to recognize that there are more and maybe additional pervasive health concerns, address our assumptions about gay men and health, and advocate for change.

Healthcare providers should be careful to examine how their own assumptions can contribute to the exclusion and dismissal of HIV-negative gay men's concerns related to autoimmune diseases. Because so much attention has been given to HIV in communities of gay men, medical professionals should be aware of and sensitive to the fact that some HIV-negative gay men with ADs may feel their health concerns are not taken as seriously. Additionally, those who are involved with healthcare should consider offering equitable services to HIV-negative and HIV-positive populations. This does not mean marginalizing the seriousness of HIV, but rather acknowledging that HIV-negative gay men with ADs may also experience similar serious complications related to their condition, and sometimes they may not have the resources or access to address them. But where HIV-positive gay men may often have access to free or discounted healthcare, medication, and even fitness centers, HIV-negative gay men with ADs are not always afforded the same. Healthcare providers should

New Directions for Adult and Continuing Education • DOI: 10.1002/ace

also exercise caution in vocalizing any assumptions they may have about their patients and work hard to create an environment where patients do not fear communicating about their ADs candidly, or even choosing to come out as gay if it is relevant.

Patient educators and patient education programs can be forces for good. Many such programs, providers, and researchers classify gay men as HIV-positive or HIV-negative, reducing the experience of being a gay man to a health and sexual behavior concern around HIV. However, being a sexual minority can be stressful. Major life events such as coming out to parents and significant others and everyday stressors caused by identity management produce illness in gay men. Stress exists for people who could be a potential target of a hate crime. This stress can cause ADs, mental health concerns, and other ailments. Because of this, patient educators should be aware that stress is as important a health concern in the gay community as HIV status.

References

Adams, J., McCreanor, T., & Braun, V. (2013). Gay men's explanations of health and how to improve it. *Qualitative Health Research*, 23(7), 887–899.

Adams, T. E. (2011). *Narrating the closet: An autoethnography of same-sex attraction.* Walnut Creek, CA: Left Coast Press.

American Autoimmune Related Diseases Association. (n.d.-a). *AARDA facts.* Retrieved from http://www.aarda.org/about-aarda/aarda-facts/

American Autoimmune Related Diseases Association. (n.d.-b). *List of autoimmune and autoimmune-related diseases.* Retrieved from http://www.aarda.org/autoimmune-information/list-of-diseases/

Burn, S. M., Kadlec, K., & Rexer, R. (2005). Effects of subtle heterosexism on gays, lesbians, and bisexuals. *Journal of Homosexuality*, 49(2), 23–38.

Calzo, J. P., Antonucci, T. C., Mays, V. M., & Cochran, S. D. (2011). Retrospective recall of sexual orientation identity development among gay, lesbian, and bisexual adults. *Developmental Psychology*, 47(6), 1658–1673.

Cohen, E. (2004). My self as an other: On autoimmunity and "other" paradoxes. *Medical Humanities*, 7, 7–11.

Delaleu, N., & Peck, A. B. (2009). Autoimmunity: Limited progress for the patient, despite decades of research. *Scandinavian Journal of Immunology*, 70(5), 411–414.

Dibble, S. L., Roberts, S. A., & Nussey, B. (2004). Comparing breast cancer risk between lesbians and their heterosexual sisters. *Women's Health Issues*, 14(2), 60–68.

Greenwood, G. L., & Gruskin, E. P. (2007). LGBT tobacco and alcohol disparities. *The Health of Sexual Minorities*, 5, 566–583.

Harcourt, J. (2006). Current issues in lesbian, gay, bisexual, and transgender (LGBT) health. *Journal of Homosexuality*, 51(1), 1–11.

Hutson, D. J. (2010). Standing OUT/fitting IN: Identity, appearance, and authenticity in gay and lesbian communities. *Symbolic Interaction*, 33(2), 213–233.

Isay, R. (2009). *Being homosexual: Gay men and their development.* New York, NY: Random House.

Jowett, A., & Peel, E. (2009). Chronic illness in non-heterosexual contexts: An online survey of experiences. *Feminism & Psychology*, 19(4), 454–474.

Kung, A. W. C. (1995). Life events, daily stresses and coping in patients with Graves' disease. *Clinical Endocrinology*, 42(3), 303–308.

Lewis, R. J., Derlega, V. J., Griffin, J. L., & Krowinski, A. C. (2003). Stressors for gay men and lesbians: Life stress, gay-related stress, stigma consciousness, and depressive symptoms. *Journal of Social and Clinical Psychology, 22*(6), 716–729.

Lipton, B. (2004). Gay men living with non-HIV chronic illnesses. *Journal of Gay and Lesbian Social Services, 17*(2), 1–23.

Meyer, I. H. (1995). Minority stress and mental health in gay men. *Journal of Health and Social Behavior, 36*(1), 38–56.

O'Leary, A. (1990). Stress, emotion, and human immune function. *Psychological Bulletin, 108*(3), 363–382.

Plummer, K. (Ed.). (2013). *Modern homosexualities: Fragments of lesbian and gay experiences.* New York, NY: Routledge.

Serefhanoglu, S., Tapan, U., Ertenli, I., Kalyoncu, U., & Uner, A. (2010). Primary thyroid marginal zone B-cell lymphoma MALT-type in a patient with rheumatoid arthritis. *Medical Oncology, 27*(3), 826–832.

Sessions, K., & Cervero, R. (2001). Solidarity and power in urban gay communities: Planning HIV prevention education. In R. M. Cervero & A. L. Wilson (Eds.), *Power in practice: Adult education and the struggle for knowledge and power in society* (pp. 247–266). San Francisco, CA: Wiley.

Smit, P. J., Brady, M., Carter, M., Fernandes, R., Lamore, L., Meulbroek, M., … Thompson, M. (2012). HIV-related stigma within communities of gay men: A literature review. *AIDS Care, 24*(4), 405–412.

Vrangalova, Z., & Savin-Williams, R. C. (2012). Mostly heterosexual and mostly gay/lesbian: Evidence for new sexual orientation identities. *Archives of Sexual Behavior, 41*(1), 85–101.

Williams Institute. (2012). *Serving our youth: Findings from a national survey of service providers working with lesbian, gay, bisexual, and transgender youth who are homeless or at risk of becoming homeless.* Retrieved from http://williamsinstitute.law.ucla.edu/wp-content/uploads/Durso-Gates-LGBT-Homeless-Youth-Survey-July-2012.pdf

Wilton, T. (1997). *Good for you: Handbook of lesbian health and wellbeing.* London, UK: Cassell.

JOSHUA C. COLLINS *is a doctoral candidate in the program for adult education and human resource development at Florida International University.*

TONETTE S. ROCCO *is a professor and program leader in the adult education and human resource development graduate program in the Department of Leadership and Professional Studies, and the director of the Office of Academic Writing and Publication Support at Florida International University.*

8

This chapter examines the challenges faced by African American women living with HIV/AIDS and how they learn to live with this chronic illness.

African American Women and HIV/AIDS

Lisa M. Baumgartner

HIV/AIDS transitioned from an acute terminal illness to a chronic disease in the United States with the advent of life-extending medications (Edelman, Gordon, & Justice, 2011). Although the phrase "AIDS crisis" is rarely heard, a crisis exists for African American women in the United States because AIDS is the third leading cause of death among that population (Henry J. Kaiser Family Foundation, 2012). Although Black women represent 12% of the population, they comprise 64% of "estimated AIDS diagnoses among women" (Henry J. Kaiser Family Foundation, 2013, para. 3) and "account for the greatest share of deaths among women with HIV in 2009 (65%)" (para. 3). The rates of HIV infection for African American women living in large cities such as Baltimore, MD, Atlanta, GA, and New York City rival rates found in the general population in the Democratic Republic of Congo (Conley, 2012).

It is important to know the challenges faced by African American women as regards HIV/AIDS. In this chapter, I discuss risk behaviors and HIV/AIDS in African American women, the sociocultural and interpersonal challenges HIV-positive African American women negotiate, and the learning that occurs as a result of living with HIV/AIDS. Last, I will provide conclusions and recommendations for health educators.

HIV/AIDS Risk Factors and African American Women

African American women face social factors such as "cultural beliefs, values and practices" that might put them more at risk for HIV/AIDS such as an imbalance in the male/female sex ratio and negative attitudes toward condom use (McNair & Prather, 2004, p. 107). Since African American women outnumber African American men, women are afraid to discuss condom use because they fear their partner might pursue relationships with women who do not insist on condom use (McNair & Prather, 2004). Scholars discovered that although African American women stated they *personally* would negotiate condom use, they believed African American women in general did not negotiate condom use because of fear of rejection from their partners (Jackson & Pittiglio, 2012).

New Directions for Adult and Continuing Education, no. 142, Summer 2014 © 2014 Wiley Periodicals, Inc.
Published online in Wiley Online Library (wileyonlinelibrary.com) • DOI: 10.1002/ace.20097

Another social factor that African American women face is having sex with men who have sex with men (MSM). In a literature review that discussed bisexual Black men, HIV risk, and heterosexual transmission, the authors found that heterosexual women might be more at risk for HIV infection from Black men who identified as gay and bisexual since 22% of gay-identified men and 61% of the bisexually identified men had had sex with a woman in the last year "compared to 12% of the heterosexually identified black MSM" (Millett, Malebranche, Mason, & Spikes, 2005, p. 54S). Black men were less likely to disclose their homosexual behavior to their heterosexual female partners (Millett et al., 2005). Although research concerning African American men on the "down low" (e.g., African American MSM who have sex with heterosexual women and do not disclose that they also have sex with men) and HIV/AIDS transmission might perpetuate racial stereotypes, conflates sexual identity with sexual behavior, and may advance the erroneous idea that Black MSM are a homogenous population (Ford, Whetten, Hall, Kaufman, & Thrasher, 2007), the fact remains that African American men on the "down low," who also have sexual relations with African American women, put the women at risk for HIV infection.

African American men on the "down low" are not the only source of HIV infection for African American women. African Americans have a smaller social network than Whites given the low male–female sex ratio due to higher rates of African American male incarceration and death (Adimora & Schoenbach, 2002). Higher reported rates of concurrent sexual relationships among heterosexual African Americans may increase infection rates among them (Adimora & Schoenbach, 2002). Additionally, African American women report higher rates of vaginal douching which increases their susceptibility to sexually transmitted diseases and may increase their chances of contracting HIV (Cottrell, 2010).

In addition to personal hygiene practices, other elements may also contribute to an increased chance of HIV infection for low-income African American women. Researchers determined that low-income African American women "who reported higher levels of fatalism, optimistic bias, interpersonal power and financial independence perceived themselves to be at less risk for HIV" (Younge, Salem, & Bybee, 2010, p. 63). Low-income African American women generally knew what put them at risk for HIV. However, an optimistic and fatalistic worldview "decrease[d] risk perception among African American women even in the face of accurate knowledge about HIV risk" (p. 67). Women tended to believe that they would not experience negative events "related to sexual behavior" (p. 67). Although fatalism (e.g., believing that a higher power controls one's health) and optimistic bias are coping mechanisms for low-income African American women in general, these traits appear to work against them as regards perceived HIV risk.

In addition to social factors, "contextual factors" or "aspects of the environment that influence an individual's perspective and therefore have import only for that person" (McNair & Prather, 2004, p. 107) place African American women at risk for HIV/AIDS. These factors include "environmental stress, relationship history, and victimization experiences" (p. 111). Scholars investigated the effect of poverty on HIV-risk factors. They found that 67% of the 524 low-income women had engaged in unwanted intercourse to avoid physical and verbal abuse, loss of shelter, or loss of relationship (Whyte, 2006). Women who engaged in unwanted sex were more likely to have unsafe sex and younger, poorer women had "higher levels of survival sex and [had] less safe sex than older women" (Whyte, 2006, p. 242). Additionally, women who had unwanted sex had a history of physical abuse by a partner and were less likely to request their partners use condoms for fear of being physically hurt (Kalichman, Williams, Cherry, Belcher, & Nachimson, 1998; Wingood & DiClemente, 1997). Women who possessed low relationship power "were far less likely to suggest condoms out of fear of partner violence, anger, and abandonment" (Harris, Gant, Pitter, & Brodie, 2009, p. 343). Additional factors that contributed to HIV risk included African Americans being more likely to live in poverty than Whites (U.S. Department of Health and Human Services, 2012), having less access to affordable healthcare (Peek et al., 2012), and African American women facing the stigmas of race, class, and gender (Berger, 2004).

African American Women's Challenges of Living With HIV/AIDS

African American women cope with factors that place them at increased risk for contracting HIV/AIDS and also face challenges in living with HIV/AIDS. In this section, I will explore how the intersections of the sociocultural context (e.g., race, class, gender, and culture) and the interpersonal context (e.g., stigma) create challenges for African American women living with HIV/AIDS (Ickovics, Thayaparan, & Ethier, 2001).

HIV-positive African American women experience multiple stigmas due to race, class, and gender. Researchers examined HIV-positive stigma discrimination among African American and White women. White women reported more HIV-related discrimination than African American women but it had no effect on measures of stress, self-esteem, and suicidal ideation (Wingood et al., 2007). In contrast, African American women who recounted HIV discrimination reported increased stress, lower self-esteem, and higher degrees of suicidal ideation. The authors posited that HIV discrimination might have been underreported by African American women due to internalized oppression, having more difficulty talking about HIV discrimination with researchers, or because African American women might have attributed their HIV-discrimination experiences to racial discrimination. The authors concluded that because African American women cope with racial discrimination and some experience poverty that "may enhance their vulnerability to the adverse health outcomes associated with HIV-discrimination" (p. 109).

New Directions for Adult and Continuing Education • DOI: 10.1002/ace

Melton (2011) noted that HIV-positive Black women were especially stigmatized because of the racist image of African American women being "sexually loose" (p. 300). Participants reported how "intersectional stigma and stereotypes" informed their experiences (p. 303). For example, a participant who lived in a drug-infested, economically challenged area of the city divulged her HIV-positive status to few people because she knew she'd be viewed as a drug addict or sex worker. Melton found that HIV-positive women were "marginalized from the margins" because revealing one's status could alienate individuals' Black female networks of friends or "'sista' circles" (p. 308). Consequently, some women did not seek HIV education or care for fear of losing their African American women support networks (Melton, 2011).

In addition to experiencing external stigma such as being seen as promiscuous, scholars discovered that African American women experienced HIV stigma internally as "existential despair" (Buseh & Stevens, 2007, p. 8). Upon diagnosis, they feared death and believed they deserved the disease. They were shunned when their status was revealed (Buseh & Stevens, 2007). Last, institutional stigma occurred when social workers, prison officials, and hospital workers treated participants disrespectfully. Strategies to resist stigma included gaining support from family and friends, finding role models who lived with the disease, using their spirituality to cope with the disease, and advocating for HIV/AIDS-related causes (Buseh & Stevens, 2007).

African American Women and Learning to Live With HIV/AIDS

Learning to live with stigma can be one aspect of learning to live with a chronic disease. As regards chronic illness, learning is implicitly and explicitly discussed in the literature. Specifically, chronically ill individuals engage in self-directed learning although African Americans' learning experiences are not the focus of the studies (Holland, 1992; Rager, 2006). Alan Tough (1971), who popularized the notion of self-directed learning, examined the self-planned learning of adults in Ontario, Canada. He discovered that adults engaged in learning projects, which he defined as "a highly deliberate effort to gain and retain certain definite knowledge and skill or to change in some way" (Tough, 1978, p. 250). Tough (1978) noted that the learning project had to be seven hours in duration and the learning sessions could occur in several episodes. Learning projects can be undertaken to "gain new knowledge, insight or understanding," to gain skills, or to change attitudes or behaviors (Tough, 1971, p. 1). Tough (1971) asserted that roughly 70% of all learning projects were planned by the learner who used individuals such as experts and media sources such as books or magazines to learn.

Like men and women living with cancer (Rager, 2006), African American women living with HIV/AIDS engaged in self-directed learning (Baumgartner, 2012). Women learned about HIV/AIDS from talking with individuals such as doctors or caseworkers or peers in HIV/AIDS support groups or seminars sponsored by AIDS Service Organizations (ASOs). Hearing others' experiences of living with HIV/AIDS was a preferred way to learn. Women read magazines, online newsletters, and websites such as the Center for Disease Control (CDC) website. Last, although her study was not framed using self-directed learning theory, Schaefer's (2005) investigation of the lived experience of fibromyalgia in African American women showed that participants engaged in self-directed learning as evidenced by searching for information about the disease on the Internet and reading books on the subject.

In addition to self-directed learning, transformative learning can occur as the result of contracting a chronic illness. Mezirow (2000) says that there can be a transformation of one's beliefs or attitudes (meaning schemes) or a transformation of one's entire worldview (perspective transformation). Mezirow (2000) delineates a 10-phase transformative learning process. Critical to this process is the presentation of a disorienting dilemma such as an HIV/AIDS diagnosis. This disorienting dilemma might prompt individuals to critically reflect on their assumptions about the world (what is really important in life?) and decide on new priorities (helping others is more important than amassing material possessions).

Although the transformative learning of individuals living with various chronic illnesses including HIV/AIDS (Courtenay, Merriam, & Reeves, 1998) and multiple sclerosis (Lewis, 2009) has been investigated, the learning experiences of people of color has not been a focus of these investigations. Regarding African Americans' experiences of chronic illness using a transformative learning framework, Ntiri and Stewart (2009) explored "the effect of an education intervention utilizing TL principles on functional health literacy and diabetes knowledge of African Americans" (p. 101). Twenty participants completed the required testing and transformative learning activity. Participants attended six diabetes education sessions, which was the transformative learning intervention, over three weeks. These course sessions motivated participants to search for more knowledge on diabetes and "to improve self-management of their illness" (p. 110).

Informal, incidental, and tacit learning can also occur for individuals living with a chronic disease. Self-directed learning is a type of informal learning where learners intentionally plan and carry out learning projects such as how to build a deck (Merriam, Caffarella, & Baumgartner, 2007). Incidental learning is accidental learning that occurs as "a by-product of doing something else" (p. 36). An example of incidental learning occurred when African American women attended an HIV/AIDS support group to learn more about how the disease was transmitted, and they met long-term survivors and realized that Persons Living with HIV/AIDS (PLWHAs) can live long, productive lives (Baumgartner, 2012). Last, tacit learning is akin to socialization and is not conscious learning although individuals might become aware of this learning at a later date (Marsick & Watkins, 1990). An example of this type of learning happened when study participants realized that ASOs and support groups socialized members into engaging in HIV/AIDS advocacy behavior (Baumgartner, 2012).

Last, individuals learned more about HIV in nonformal settings. Nonformal educational opportunities are "learning opportunities *outside* the formal educational system" (italics in original) and they generally have a curriculum and a facilitator (Merriam et al., 2007, p. 30). HIV/AIDS education programs, HIV/AIDS support groups, and group meetings for recovering addicts living with HIV/AIDS are examples of nonformal education. Since the sample was solicited from ASOs, all participants engaged in nonformal education through support groups and HIV/AIDS trainings at ASOs (Baumgartner, 2012).

Conclusions and Recommendations

Living and learning with HIV/AIDS occurs in community. Various contexts including interpersonal (e.g., stigma and support) and sociocultural (e.g., race, class, gender, and culture) affect individuals' experiences of living with HIV/AIDS in the community (Ickovics et al., 2001). Women experience multiple stigmas because of their race, gender, socioeconomic status, and HIV-positive status in the community. However, support services that cater to PLWHAs can mitigate some of that stigma.

Scholars assert that "framing institutions" (Watkins-Hayes, Pittman-Gay, & Beaman, 2012, p. 2028) and "framing agents" (p. 2032) within those institutions greatly influence how African American women cope with HIV/AIDS. Framing institutions "generate language, adaptive skills, and practical knowledge that shape how individuals interpret a new life condition and whether they ultimately see it as a platform for growth" (p. 2030) and include hospitals, clinics, and prisons. Framing agents are "actors within these institutions who individually inform how illness is constructed and addressed, offering explicit and implicit directives for coping" (p. 2030) and include nurses, doctors, and other healthcare professionals. Framing institutions "operate as intermediaries between micro-level perceptions and actions and macro-structural forces and systems positioned between one's personal response to a new circumstance and the larger set of privileges and disadvantages that she experiences due to [African American women's] social location" (p. 2030). Researchers interviewed 30 African American women living with HIV/AIDS and found that framing agents and institutions affected how individuals coped immediately after diagnosis and how newly diagnosed participants conceptualized HIV/AIDS (Watkins-Hayes et al., 2012). Framing institutions helped participants learn how to talk about their disease and provided access to resources. Some framing institutions helped participants see their diagnosis in a positive light. African American women less tied to framing agents did not cope as well with HIV/AIDS (Watkins-Hayes et al., 2012). Alternatively, some framing agents did not frame the disease positively (e.g., telling prisoners to remain silent about their diagnosis) which caused participants to engage in maladaptive coping behaviors (Watkins-Hayes et al., 2012).

Depending on how issues regarding living with HIV/AIDS are addressed, framing institutions and framing agents can either empower or disempower

PLWHAs (Watkins-Hayes et al., 2012). It is important that ASOs recognize the multiple stigmas that African American women contend with in order to provide support services for them. For example, support groups that cater to African American women and issues particular to them are needed. Further, programs that focus on sexual assertiveness as regards condom use and the availability of counseling sessions for women who have experienced sexual and physical abuse are needed so women can be empowered to take charge of their intimate relationships with others.

Given that low relationship power predicted a lack of condom negotiation, Harris et al. (2009) recommend that prevention programs should focus on helping women "cognitively restructure the way they approach and define power within their interpersonal relationships with men" (p. 345). High relationship power led to "incredibly powerful reductions in HIV risk and it explains 40% of variance in perceived HIV risk behavior" (p. 346).

Regarding learning, it is clear HIV-positive African American women engage in nonformal education, and self-directed and incidental learning. Many prefer learning about HIV/AIDS from others although they also utilize print materials and the Internet (Baumgartner, 2012). Framing institutions should know that peer support groups, groups led by professionals, and guest speakers are preferred ways for African American women to learn about HIV/AIDS. Seeing and hearing from long-term survivors was especially helpful to HIV-positive African American women.

Last, additional research is needed in a variety of areas. First, additional research is needed to determine whether HIV infection among heterosexual African American women is driven by a smaller group of bisexual HIV-positive men whose risk behavior is unknown or a large group of "exclusively heterosexual black men who have comparatively lower HIV prevalence but high HIV risk behavior" (Millett et al., 2005, p. 57S). Second, there is a dearth of research on the experiences of PLWHAs living in rural areas including African American women. Findings from this research could add depth to the extant literature. Third, community-based participatory research has been lauded as a potentially effective research methodology for studies concerning HIV/AIDS prevention, care, and treatment (Rhodes, Malow, & Jolly, 2010). However, more studies using this methodology are needed that discuss the concerns of African American women.

In sum, African American women are more at risk for contracting HIV/AIDS than women from other demographics. They also face special challenges in living with HIV/AIDS in a racist, sexist, and classist society. "Framing institutions" (Watkins-Hayes et al., 2012, p. 2028) such as ASOs and hospitals and "framing agents" (p. 2028) such as social workers and HIV/AIDS educators can provide the language and support necessary for individuals to transition from thinking they will die from HIV/AIDS to living with HIV/AIDS (Watkins-Hayes et al., 2012). HIV/AIDS educators need to recognize the challenging conditions under which African American women live with HIV/AIDS and provide learning opportunities tailored to their preferences. Last, HIV-positive

African American women might be underrepresented at the planning table when various "framing institutions" (Watkins-Hayes et al., 2012, p. 2028) convene program planning meetings, and their voices need to be heard.

References

Adimora, A. A., & Schoenbach, V. J. (2002). Contextual factors and the Black–White disparity in heterosexual HIV transmission. *Epidemiology and Society, 13*, 707–712.

Baumgartner, L. M. (2012). *African American women's experiences of learning to live with HIV/AIDS.* Unpublished manuscript.

Berger, M. T. (2004). *Workable sisterhood: The political journey of stigmatized women with HIV/AIDS.* Princeton, NJ: Princeton University Press.

Buseh, A. G., & Stevens, P. E. (2007). Constrained but not determined by stigma: Resistance by African American women living with HIV. *Women & Health, 44*(3), 1–18. doi:10.1300/J013v44n03_01

Conley, M. (2012, March 9). *Shocking HIV rates among Black women: Study.* Retrieved from http://abcnews.go.com/Health/AIDS/hiv-rates-black-urban-women-times-higher -previously/story?id=15878578

Cottrell, B. H. (2010). An updated review of evidence to discourage douching. *MCN: The American Journal of Maternal and Child Nursing, 35*(2), 102 107. doi:10.1097/NMC.0b013e3181cae9da

Courtenay, B. C., Merriam, S. B., & Reeves, P. M. (1998). The centrality of meaning-making in transformational learning: How HIV-positive adults make sense of their lives. *Adult Education Quarterly, 48*, 65–84. doi:10.1177/074171369804800203

Edelman, E. J., Gordon, K., & Justice, A. C. (2011). Patient and provider-reported symptoms in the Post-cART Era. *AIDS and Behavior, 15*, 853–861. doi:10.1007/s10461-010 -9706-z

Ford, C. L., Whetten, K. D., Hall, S. A., Kaufman, J. S., & Thrasher, A. D. (2007). Black sexuality, social construction, and research targeting 'The Down Low' ('The DL'). *Annals of Epidemiology, 17*, 206–216. doi:10.1016/j.annepidem.2006.09.006

Harris, K. A., Gant, L. M., Pitter, R., & Brodie, D. A. (2009). Associations between HIV risk, unmitigated communion and relationship power among African American women. *Journal of HIV /AIDS & Social Services, 8*, 331–351. doi:10.1080/15381500903396865

Henry J. Kaiser Family Foundation. (2012). *Black Americans and HIV/AIDS.* Retrieved from http://www.kff.org/hivaids/upload/6089-09.pdf

Henry J. Kaiser Family Foundation. (2013). *Women and HIV/AIDS in the United States.* Retrieved from http://www.kff.org/hivaids/upload/6092-11.pdf

Holland, N. (1992). *Self-directed learning in individuals with multiple sclerosis* (Unpublished doctoral dissertation). Teachers College, Columbia University.

Ickovics, J. R., Thayaparan, B., & Ethier, K. A. (2001). Women and AIDS: A contextual analysis. In A. Baum, T. A. Revenson, & J. E. Singer (Eds.), *Handbook of health psychology* (pp. 817–839). Mahwah, NJ: Erlbaum.

Jackson, F., & Pittiglio, L. (2012). Reducing HIV in Michigan African American young adult women. *Journal of the Association of Nurses in AIDS Care, 23*, 521–530. doi:10.1016/j.jana.2011.12.005

Kalichman, S. C., Williams, E. A., Cherry, C., Belcher, L., & Nachimson, D. (1998). Sexual coercion, domestic violence and negotiating condom use among low-income African American women. *Journal of Women's Health, 7*, 371–378. doi:10.1089/jwh.1998.7.371

Lewis, M. (2009). *Transformative learning in the multiple sclerosis community: An ethnographic study examining how and in what ways transformative learning is realized and lived among members of an MS community* (Unpublished doctoral dissertation). National Louis University, Chicago, IL.

Marsick, V. J., & Watkins, K. (1990). *Informal and incidental learning in the workplace.* New York, NY: Routledge.

McNair, L. D., & Prather, C. M. (2004). African American women and AIDS: Factors influencing risk and reaction to HIV disease. *Journal of Black Psychology, 30,* 106–123. doi:10.1177/0095798403261414

Melton, M. L. (2011). Sex, lies and stereotypes: HIV positive Black women's perspectives on HIV stigma and the need for public policy as HIV/AIDS prevention intervention. *Race, Gender and Class, 18,* 295–313.

Merriam, S. B., Caffarella, R. S., & Baumgartner, L. M. (2007). *Learning in adulthood: A comprehensive guide* (3rd ed.). San Francisco, CA: Jossey-Bass.

Mezirow, J. (2000). Learning to think like an adult: Core concepts of transformation theory. In J. Mezirow and Associates (Eds.), *Learning as transformation: Critical perspectives on a theory in progress* (pp. 3–33). San Francisco, CA: Jossey-Bass.

Millett, G., Malebranche, D., Mason, B., & Spikes, P. (2005). Focusing "down low": Bisexual black men, HIV risk and heterosexual transmission. *Journal of the National Medical Association, 97*(7), 52S–59S.

Ntiri, D. W., & Stewart, M. (2009). Transformative learning intervention: Effect on functional health literacy and diabetes knowledge in older African Americans. *Gerontology and Geriatrics Education, 30,* 100–113. doi:10.1080/0270196092911265

Peek, M. E., Wilson, S. C., Bussy-Jones, J., Lypson, M., Cardasco, K., Jacobs, E. A., ... Brown, A. F. (2012). A study of national physician organizations' efforts to reduce racial and ethnic health disparities in the United States. *Academic Medicine, 87*(6), 694–700. doi:10.1097/ACM.0b013e318253b074

Rager, K. (2006). Self-directed learning and prostate cancer: A thematic analysis of the experiences of twelve patients. *International Journal of Qualitative Studies in Education, 25,* 447–461. doi:10.1080/02601370600911982

Rhodes, S. D., Malow, R. M., & Jolly, C. (2010). Community-based participatory research: A new and not-so-new approach to HIV/AIDS prevention, care, and treatment. *AIDS Education and Prevention, 22*(3), 173–183.

Schaefer, K. M. (2005). The lived experience of fibromyalgia in African American women. *Holistic Nursing Practice, 19,* 17–25.

Tough, A. (1971). *The adult's learning projects: A fresh approach to theory and practice in adult learning.* Toronto, Ontario: Ontario Institution of Studies in Education.

Tough, A. (1978). Major learning efforts: Recent research and future directions. *Adult Education, 28,* 250–263.

U.S. Department of Health and Human Services. (2012). *Information on poverty and income statistics: A summary of 2012 current population survey data.* Retrieved from http://aspe.hhs.gov/hsp/12/povertyandincomeest/ib.shtml

Watkins-Hayes, C., Pittman-Gay, L., & Beaman, J. (2012). 'Dying from' to 'living with': Framing institutions and the coping processes of African American women living with HIV/AIDS. *Social Science and Medicine, 74,* 2028–2036. doi:10.1016/j.socscimed.2012.02.001

Whyte, J. (2006). Sexual assertiveness in low-income African American women: Unwanted sex, survival and HIV-risk. *Journal of Community Health Nursing, 23*(4), 235–244. doi:10.1207/s15327655jchn2304_4

Wingood, G. M., & DiClemente, R. J. (1997). The effects of an abusive primary partner on the condom use and sexual negotiation practices of African-American women. *American Journal of Public Health, 87,* 1016–1018. doi:10.2105/AJPH.87.6.1016

Wingood, G. M., DiClemente, R. J., Mikhail, I., McCree, D. H., Davies, S. L., Hardin, J. W., ... Saag, M. (2007). HIV discrimination and the health of women living with HIV. *Women and Health, 46,* 99–112. doi:10.1300/J013v46n02_07

Younge, S. N., Salem, D., & Bybee, D. (2010). Risk revisited: The perception of HIV risk in a community sample of low income African American women. *Journal of Black Psychology*, *36*, 49–74.

LISA M. BAUMGARTNER *is an associate professor in the adult education and human resource development program in the Department of Educational Administration and Human Resource Development at Texas A&M University.*

New Directions for Adult and Continuing Education • DOI: 10.1002/ace

9

Oppression in its many forms is so ingrained in the fabric of the legal, social, economic, educational, political, and medical systems in America that it often goes unrecognized and unaddressed. The chapters in this volume explored the evasive problem of health and wellness for racial, ethnic, and sexual minorities within a framework of adult education principles.

Partnerships and Collaborations in Promoting Health and Wellness in Minority Communities: Lessons Learned and Future Directions

Lawrence O. Bryant

Many formative players shaped the framework of adult education from a historical perspective. I would be remiss if I did not acknowledge the work of Paolo Freire. His landmark, *Pedagogy of the Oppressed*, harkens adult educators to empower the oppressed and the marginalized by challenging the forces of oppression (Freire, 1970). Other adult educators have addressed issues related to race, gender, and sexual orientation within the last 10 years. Scholars such as Juanita Johnson-Bailey, Phyllis Cunningham, and Robert J. Hill have vociferously challenged racism, sexism, patriarchy, and heterosexism in their substantive body of work. Additionally, Johnson-Bailey has examined the intersection between race and gender, Cunningham has challenged hegemony, managerial control, and dehumanization at every turn, and Hill (2003) has long been an advocate for sexual minorities. Hill further asserted that "Topics of interest in minority communities cover a wide range of issues; including, legal advice, health and wellness education, women's advocacy; drug and alcohol abuse education, personal development and safer sex education" (p. 107). In conversation during my dissertation defense, committee members Talmadge Guy and Juanita Johnson-Bailey encouraged my continued work in challenging homophobia and racism, beyond just my dissertation (Bryant, 2008). They provided examples of how, as an adult educator and a registered respiratory therapist, I could begin to make inroads in working with the sexual minority population as it relates to health disparities and health equity (T. Guy & J. Johnson-Bailey, personal communication, May 2008). This

NEW DIRECTIONS FOR ADULT AND CONTINUING EDUCATION, no. 142, Summer 2014 © 2014 Wiley Periodicals, Inc.
Published online in Wiley Online Library (wileyonlinelibrary.com) • DOI: 10.1002/ace.20098

encouragement sets the stage for my current health disparities work with sexual minority communities related to tobacco control (Bryant, Bowman, & Damarin, 2011). These examples provide evidence that adult educators can support minority health and wellness, self-actualization, and promote social change. However, as you will see throughout the pages of these chapters, the stench of oppression frequently displaces minority populations from resources and attention needed for health and wellness (Malebranche, Fields, Bryant, & Harper, 2007).

Health, Wellness, and Minority Communities

Given the many preventable diseases in racial, ethnic, and sexual minority communities, health and wellness is essential to our nation's overall well-being. Chapter authors in this volume agree that minority populations experience health-related disparities, which adversely impact their health and wellness. Diseases such as HIV/AIDS, tuberculosis, addiction, and smoking-related disorders disproportionately impact minority communities. For example, Baumgartner (Chapter 8) illustrates how minority women experience disproportionate rates of HIV/AIDS. Baumgartner asserts that minority women struggle with social conditions such as poverty, income inequality, and unemployment, which make it more difficult to protect their sexual health.

Health and wellness concerns for racial, ethnic, and sexual minorities are inseparable from larger social issues such as racism, discrimination, and homophobia. These concerns prompted Egan (Chapter 4) to boldly challenge established social norms regarding health. His chapter reminds us that oppression and discrimination are without borders. He states that the Aboriginal community of Canada is still recovering from over 500 years of genocide and state-sponsored discrimination; this oppression has adversely affected their health. Egan also calls attention to the disproportionate rate of HIV/AIDS among members of the Aboriginal community. He has worked tirelessly in partnership with community-based organizations to promote ways in which more mainstream ideas about knowledge could be aligned with challenging and disrupting power, in the forms of homophobia and heteronormativity. It is exactly this type of social justice and social action that we argue positions adult educators as powerful catalysts for social change.

Lessons Learned

Each chapter has provided a plethora of ideas and recommendations for how adult educators can inform both research and practice in dealing with racial and sexual minorities as it relates to their health. The authors have conceptualized education and learning as an important element in maintaining health and wellness.

Adult educators possess insights and skills that are crucial in helping adults learn about disease treatment and prevention. The authors in this volume describe how partnerships and collaboration in cooperation with minority communities in churches, community centers, and support groups provide unique opportunities to improve health outcomes. Merriam, Caffarella, and Baumgartner (2007) contend that learning opportunities outside the formal education settings may enhance and complement the needs of underserved adults. They point out that with its flexibility and fluid structure nonformal education is appropriate in dealing with inequalities, injustices, discrimination, and oppression of marginal communities. In other words, minority communities can provide opportunities for adult educators to identify resources where effective learning and research can take place.

In Chapter 1, Collins and Rocco provide examples of how racial, ethnic, and sexual minority communities may utilize already existing resources in promoting identity development at the intersection of health and wellness. They acknowledge that places like schools, religious institutions, families, community-based organizations, and other gathering places provide opportunities for adult educators to partner in helping deal with the many social issues minority communities face. Rowland and Isaac-Savage (Chapter 2) expound on the important role of the Black church, as a religious institution and community-based organization, in eradicating the extant disparities of African Americans. They explore many factors that contribute to health disparities among African Americans. These factors include inadequate access to care, poor quality of care, poverty, violence, and personal behaviors. Hence, the Black church can help bridge the disparity gap in ethnic minority communities. The authors of this chapter further remind us that in collaborating with the church adult educators can play an extensive role in developing healthcare initiatives and programs that can reduce the impact of health disparities and assist in the design and implementation of programs that address diseases disproportionately affecting them.

More in-depth discussions on community collaborations and partnerships are found in Chapters 3 and 4. In Chapter 3, Prins and Mooney demonstrate how collaborations and partnerships can increase health literacy. Community-based organizations and adult educators can address health literacy by developing partnerships with institutions such as healthcare centers and physician groups. Egan, in Chapter 4, reports positive outcomes in his collaboration with community organizations such as the Canadian Aboriginal AIDS Network (CAAN). Since this organization could not apply for funding on its own, it partnered with adult educators from a local university. Egan also informs us that being a community partner is not always about agreeing or acquiescing; he states that at times he has had to assert himself and to challenge established norms. He further acknowledges that this partnership, while invoking an indigenous epistemology, resulted in rigorous results at the intersection of power and knowledge.

Gedro (Chapter 5) discusses factors affecting lesbians and alcoholism. Because bars are central to social life in the gay community, these smoke- and alcohol-filled venues are where many lesbian, gay, bisexual, and transgender

(LGBT) adopt unhealthy lifestyle behaviors. Because tobacco is a contributing factor in poor health, Bryant and Bowman's discussion on these issues in Chapter 6 points out that smoking is a significant factor in perpetuating preventable diseases among LGBT communities. In Chapter 7, Collins and Rocco discuss how dialogue and action within sexual minority communities can sometimes silence certain issues while emphasizing and even perpetuating stereotypes regarding other issues. Baumgartner (Chapter 8) eloquently presents a similar argument addressing how African American women are often pushed to the margins of conversation regarding HIV/AIDS, though they are disproportionally affected by the disease. All authors poignantly provide examples of how adult educators, in promoting social justice and inclusion, can help transform negative societal attitudes toward minorities and collaborate with community leaders to extinguish the flames of oppression. As health disparities exist among all racial, ethnic, and sexual minorities, adult educators can serve as social action agents of change and begin to work collaboratively with minority communities in promoting health and wellness.

Future Directions

Promoting the health and wellness of minorities is a social justice and human rights issue. In a groundbreaking speech to the opening session of the *13th Annual Creating Change Conference*, organized by the National Gay and Lesbian Task Force, Coretta Scott King made her now famous appeal linking the Civil Rights Movement to the LGBT Human Rights Movement, with the following sweeping call to action: "I appeal to everyone who believes in Martin Luther King Jr.'s dream to make room at the table of brotherhood and sisterhood for lesbian and gay people . . ." (King, 2000, para. 4). Through inclusion, social action, and social justice, adult educators can bridge the health and wellness gap among minorities. Adult educators possess the abilities, knowledge, and skills needed to trouble the waters of oppression and discrimination. Within our extensive archive of research and programmatic expertise, adult educators can utilize strategies such as transformative learning, program planning, nonformal education, and social learning to promote efficacious and evidence-based programs and projects in partnership with minority communities.

Historically, adult educators have been on the front lines of social justice issues, from the civil rights movement to women's rights, adult educators have provided evidence-based insights that have proven effectiveness. It is this commitment to justice that a better and more inclusive world can finally be realized for all communities.

References

Bryant, L. (2008). *How Black men who have sex with men learn to cope with homophobia and racism* (Unpublished doctoral dissertation). University of Georgia, Athens, GA.

Bryant, L., Bowman, L., & Damarin, A. (2011). Assessment for a better understanding of tobacco use by LGBT Atlantans. *Respiratory Care Education Annual*, *20*, 63–73.

Freire, P. (1970). *Pedagogy of the oppressed.* New York, NY: Continuum.

Hill, R. (2003). Turning a gay gaze on citizenship. Sexual orientation and gender identity: Contesting/ed terrain. In C. Medel-Anonuevo & G. Mitchell (Eds.), *Citizenship, democracy and lifelong learning* (pp. 99–139). Hamburg, Germany: The United Nations Educational, Scientific, & Cultural Organization (UNESCO), Institute for Education (UIE). Retrieved from http://www.unesco.org/education/uie/pdf/uiestud35.pdf

King, C. S. (2000, November). *Remarks at the 13th Annual Creating a Change Conference on lesbian, gay, bisexual, transgender: Human rights and other issues.* Retrieved from http://www.seympeace.org/CSKing.htm

Malebranche, D., Fields, L., Bryant, L., & Harper, S. (2007). Cool pose revisited: The social context of masculinity and sexual risk among Black men who have sex with men. *Men and Masculinity*, Article 10.1177. Retrieved from http://jmm.sagepub.com/cgi/rapidpdf/1097184×07309504v1

Merriam, S. B., Caffarella, R., & Baumgartner, L. (2007). *Learning in adulthood: A comprehensive guide.* San Francisco, CA: Jossey-Bass.

Lawrence O. Bryant is an assistant professor at Georgia State University, Byrdine Lewis School of Nursing and Health Profession, Department of Respiratory Therapy.

Index

NEW DIRECTIONS FOR ADULT AND CONTINUING EDUCATION
ORDER FORM SUBSCRIPTION AND SINGLE ISSUES

DISCOUNTED BACK ISSUES:

Use this form to receive 20% off all back issues of *New Directions for Adult and Continuing Education*.
All single issues priced at **$23.20** (normally $29.00)

TITLE	ISSUE NO.	ISBN
_____	_____	_____
_____	_____	_____
_____	_____	_____

*Call 888-378-2537 or see mailing instructions below. When calling, mention the promotional code JBNND
to receive your discount. For a complete list of issues, please visit www.josseybass.com/go/ndace*

SUBSCRIPTIONS: (1 YEAR, 4 ISSUES)

☐ New Order   ☐ Renewal

U.S.	☐ Individual: $89	☐ Institutional: $311
CANADA/MEXICO	☐ Individual: $89	☐ Institutional: $351
ALL OTHERS	☐ Individual: $113	☐ Institutional: $385

*Call 888-378-2537 or see mailing and pricing instructions below.
Online subscriptions are available at www.onlinelibrary.wiley.com*

ORDER TOTALS:

Issue / Subscription Amount: $ _____

Shipping Amount: $ _____
(for single issues only – subscription prices include shipping)

Total Amount: $ _____

SHIPPING CHARGES:

First Item	$6.00
Each Add'l Item	$2.00

*(No sales tax for U.S. subscriptions. Canadian residents, add GST for subscription orders. Individual rate subscriptions must
be paid by personal check or credit card. Individual rate subscriptions may not be resold as library copies.)*

BILLING & SHIPPING INFORMATION:

☐ **PAYMENT ENCLOSED:** *(U.S. check or money order only. All payments must be in U.S. dollars.)*

☐ **CREDIT CARD:**   ☐ VISA   ☐ MC   ☐ AMEX

Card number _____Exp. Date_____

Card Holder Name_____Card Issue # _____

Signature _____Day Phone_____

☐ **BILL ME:** *(U.S. institutional orders only. Purchase order required.)*

Purchase order # _____
Federal Tax ID 13559302 • GST 89102-8052

Name_____

Address_____

Phone_____ E-mail_____

Copy or detach page and send to: **John Wiley & Sons, One Montgomery Street, Suite 1200,
San Francisco, CA 94104-4594**

Order Form can also be faxed to: **888-481-2665**

PROMO JBNND